PERSUADED

PERSUADED

The Communication Strategy that Builds Credibility, Forges Connections, Inspires Action, and Helps You Succeed

Dean M. Brenner

PERSUASION

PUBLISHING

Wallingford, CT

Persuaded: The Communication Strategy that Builds Credibility, Forges Connections, Inspires Action, and Helps You Succeed

Published by Persuasion Publishing
350 Center Place Suite 106
Wallingford, CT 06492
Copyright © 2020 by Dean M. Brenner

Library of Congress Control Number: 2020939048

ISBN (hardcover): 9781662901584
eISBN:9781662901607

This book is written in honor of and with deep gratitude for Kent Brittan, a great and kind man and an even greater friend. We were introduced by a mutual acquaintance in 2003 and, soon after, Kent gave me and The Latimer Group our first significant client opportunity—a major leap of faith for which I am forever grateful. Without that leap of faith, the entire trajectory of The Latimer Group would look very different.

I think about you, Kent, every day, and I will spend the rest of my life trying to replicate your generosity in the way I treat my clients, friends, and colleagues.

Contents

Foreword

Throughout my thirty-five-year career at United Technologies, Sikorsky Aircraft, and FedEx, I have learned over and over again that there are a few essential skills for success. Every leader needs to be able to set a vision and a direction for the organization, assemble a team of talented and committed individuals, and communicate clearly and effectively to all of her constituents. All three skills are required. But when I am giving advice to young, emerging leaders, I always make it clear that while great leadership requires a number of skills, effective communication skills make everything else easier. If you can communicate really well, you can accomplish almost anything. When you can't, you will almost certainly find success elusive.

When I think about the best and worst leadership moments in my career, the common denominator in every story has been communication. When I am communicating well—listening, planning, speaking—the story almost always ends well. When I neglect my communication, the story almost always ends poorly. There is no doubt in my mind that communication skills have had an indelible impact on my career.

Let's take this even further. The value of great communication skills goes well beyond the individual—the same holds true for the entire organization. An organization that values, teaches, and reinforces great communication aligns and motivates its workforce, satisfies its customers, and surpasses its goals. I have had the honor of working for some outstanding organizations during my career, and each of them has valued great communication skills. Those exceptional organizations thrive when each individual embraces the fundamentals of strong communication (listening, thoughtful planning, and clear delivery) *and when the organization embraces and reinforces those fundamentals.* When leadership is committed and creates accountability, great communication becomes part of the fabric of the organization. It gets embedded in the DNA, and that leads to stronger teams and better outcomes, which ultimately helps the bottom line.

People and organizations have to be good at a lot of things—communication may be at the top of the list, but it is a long list. Which means that the skills being taught need to be easily *and quickly* applicable and usable. The approach to communication must be easy to absorb and apply, so that it can be used over and over within the time restrictions of the modern business world. In this book, Dean lays out just such a system. He is not just teaching great communication skills in this book. He is teaching those skills in a way that even the busiest people will find valuable.

I believe that you will find the ideas contained inside *Persuaded* to be immensely valuable to you and your organization. My hope is that after reading this book, you will be inspired to make communication skills a primary focus in your career development. Trust me…you won't regret it.

Susan Spence
Vice President of Sourcing and Procurement
FedEx

Author's Note

Like most of us, there are multiple sides to me and my story. On one hand, I am highly performance-oriented, and care deeply about data and metrics. I love to compete. I was an Olympic-caliber sailor and then the team leader for two Olympic sailing teams. There is a big part of my brain that is highly quantitative, and that is wired to care about wins and losses.

But on the other hand, I love connecting with people—engaging in conversation, or just being present, with people I enjoy. The relationships in my life give me energy and purpose, and there is little that makes me happier than seeing someone I care about thrive. If I can help a little along the way, even better. In other words, I also have a highly qualitative side.

For the longest time, I always assumed that these two sides of my brain were essentially going to be in conflict with each other—that my urge to compete would always bump into my urge to connect. It is hard to consistently connect with people that you are also trying to defeat.

But eventually there was a realization, an epiphany really, sparked by my wife Emily, the great love of my life. We were hiking on the Bright Angel Trail in the Grand Canyon in the fall of 2000. Over the course of many hikes that fall, we had been examining what would come next in our lives, and my next professional pursuit was the most perplexing question in front of us. But then Emily observed, in an almost exasperated tone, "Dean, you love to coach and teach, you are a good public speaker, and you love to connect with people. Build a business around those three things. Bring those things together."

In my experience, most of the great ideas tend to come out in the simplest ways, usually during conversation with a trusted voice. Emily had identified for me that there was a way to bring my quantitative self together with my qualitative self. In so doing, I could build something that would allow people to think about communication in a new way. And right there, the idea for The Latimer Group emerged.

Since then, The Latimer Group has expanded to, as of this writing, a group of six outstanding colleagues. Along the way, we have remained committed to that original vision. This book and this company are based on a simple and powerful idea—that great communication skills can change the world. Everything that The Latimer Group does derives from the mission of helping people and organizations communicate clearly, powerfully, and persuasively.

Beneath that mission are three core ideas:

- First, communication springs from connection. And connecting to others—with curiosity, empathy, and respect—allows us to bridge differences and open dialogue, create solutions, and forge paths into the future.
- Second, communication is not the "soft skill" that so many people misunderstand it to be. Good communication, especially in the modern business environment, is a requirement. There is nothing "soft" about this skill.
- Third, communication skills are not exclusively innate. They can be learned, practiced, and developed. We live in a crowded, noisy, complicated world. Everyone is busy. Every organization is trying to do many things at once. We are all overwhelmed with information

and access to our time from others. So, the ability to capture attention and get people to listen to you in the first place takes some work.

But we at The Latimer Group believe that the solutions to these challenges lie in the simplest of ideas. We believe that things like listening, empathy, respect, awareness, preparation, and practice create the opportunity to connect with others and communicate well. We believe that *everyone* has the ability to communicate clearly and persuasively. Our job is to make that easier and more accessible for you.

That is the promise of this book. Good luck!

– *Dean Brenner*

A Note on the Text

I use many stories throughout the book to illustrate The Latimer Group's techniques and concepts. While all of these stories have been drawn from my team's experience in coaching and speaking, I have changed identifying names and details to protect the identities of individuals and companies. Additionally, some stories are composites of two or more real events.

Portions of the material in this book have been previously published, in slightly different form, at Forbes.com and The Latimer Group blog at www.TheLatimerGroup.com.

Introduction

ELIMINATING THE MESSENGER MINDSET

Think about a literal messenger—say, someone who is delivering packages. Once he's dropped off a package and gotten the signature he needs, he doesn't care what the person receiving the package does with it—whether she opens it and loves what's inside, or hates what it contains, or just throws the package out without opening it at all. That has nothing to do with the delivery of the package. Once the package is handed off, the messenger has fulfilled his value proposition and done his job.

In communication, to be a messenger is to think that our primary job is to inform, update, or share. But in purposeful communication, we must care what our audience does with the package we are delivering to them: our message. We must consider how our message will be received, and whether the message produces the outcome we want. We have to be more than a messenger.

Changing your mindset is step one of preparing to communicate. If we are in messenger mode, we end our inquiry with a period: here's what I need to say, full stop. This mindset puts us in what sailors or truckers, in using handheld radios, call "transmit-only mode." We are limiting our communication to a one-way approach of information distribution.

But what happens if, instead of ending our inquiry with a period, we use a comma and a question mark? Here's what

I need to say, *and* what will my audience think of it? What do they need to hear? What do I *want* them to think? How do I use my skills to persuade them? What is the larger context in which this meeting is taking place? Instead of being in "transmit-only mode," we have now turned that handheld radio into a tool for two-way communication. We care about distributing and receiving information.

To communicate well, we need empathy: to understand our audience and be aware of their goals and constraints. We need to engage: to understand that communication isn't a one-way flow of information, but a dialogue—conceptually, if not literally. We need curiosity: what can your audience tell you about themselves? And how difficult is the challenge facing us? After all, there's a difference between asking someone to support a small change that requires little investment and an incremental change of mindset and asking for thousands or hundreds of thousands of dollars in budget and a major change in strategy.

So how do you break out of the messenger mindset and set off down the path of speaking persuasively?

First, approach communication with the right attitude, one that recognizes that every communication is an opportunity to persuade.

Second, commit to the process. Take the time you need to practice your skills as a speaker. Don't be afraid to challenge yourself.

Third, seek out learning opportunities. Volunteer to speak in meetings. Ask for feedback (and give feedback in return). Find a mentor.

Fourth, develop a curiosity about other perspectives, and what others might think about your topic. Train yourself to think beyond your own perspective.

The challenge might seem overwhelming. But, like any skill, effective communication isn't monolithic; it is an accumulation of smaller skill sets, each of which can be understood and practiced on its own. This book shows you the Latimer Model, a series of skill-building strategies that, when put together, can eliminate the messenger mindset and create a more persuasive speaker and leader.

End the Suffering

Do any of these scenarios sound familiar?

You've spent days preparing for a big meeting with your boss. You've gathered all the relevant data, put together a comprehensive slide deck, and now you're in the room. But you've just started presenting your numbers when you notice that your boss has her phone out, typing emails and scrolling through her feed. All your carefully curated detail—she's not hearing any of it.

*

At your company, almost every day has at least one meeting scheduled, and often you spend half the day shuffling from one conference room to another. Most of the meetings take twice as long as they should, little consensus is formed, and you all leave the room exhausted and without resolution.

*

You are part of a team that has several members that work remotely. When you try to get things done or pursue initiatives, getting everyone on the same page feels impossible. Half of the time, no one really seems to understand the team goals or who is responsible for what. When you schedule a conference call, it's clear that everyone is multitasking throughout the conversation, and it's difficult to capture anyone's full attention. It seems impossible to find a way to stay focused and inspired, and each team member feels isolated, unmotivated, and stressed out.

I am confident that most of us have experienced a situation similar to one of these at some point in our working lives. For some of us, these types of challenges represent day-to-day life in the office. What's the common thread? Poor communication.

We live and work in a world in which access to information is immediate, voluminous, and incessant—but understanding what it *means* can be elusive. We can communicate with each other face-to-face, over email, by phone, by Skype, by text, by IM, by Slack. Yet, overwhelmed by the options, sometimes we fail to communicate at all. Instant gratification is ubiquitous; we never have to wait for the cliffhanger to be resolved because every episode is available right now—and that means that binging, tell-me-*right-now* is the default mode of consuming information. We can easily connect with someone who lives on the other side of the world—but we feel totally disconnected from the people on the other side of the cubicle wall.

All of these problems, at base, are communication problems. When we don't communicate well, we feel drained and demoralized and we lose sight of our common goals. Business stagnates. We feel overworked and underachieving. We feel disconnected from our leadership and our peers.

And we feel these problems outside of the workplace, too. We live in a political landscape in which two sides can barely agree on reality, much less find practical solutions to the many urgent problems that face us. The ease and anonymity of social media allows insults rather than engagement. Even as technology makes us available to everyone, all the time, more people report feeling isolated than ever before—what's been called a loneliness epidemic. (According to a poll conducted by *The Economist* and the Kaiser Family Foundation, more than 20 percent of adults in the US and the UK report feeling socially isolated often or all of the time.) We are in a crisis of communication in all aspects of our lives.

But there is a solution. We need to approach the way we communicate mindfully, giving ourselves time to reflect and prepare, and treating whomever we are speaking with respectfully. We need to take deliberate steps to improve our skills. That's where this book and the Latimer Model come in: a focused, piece-by-piece, and measurable way to speak more clearly, concisely, and persuasively. By breaking down the specific skills that go into effective communication, this model gives you a way to efficiently and successfully practice and implement better communication.

When we communicate well, we can hold our audience's attention, synthesize information and present it clearly, choose the right venue, and get straight to the point. When we communicate well, we *connect* well. We not only inform—we engage and we *inspire*.

THE LATIMER GROUP MODEL
Breaking Down Communication to Build Up Persuasion

The most important part of becoming a better communicator is to recognize that persuasive communication is not a single, one-dimensional skill: it is the sum total of several distinct strategies and skills that can each be practiced and improved on their own as well as welded together as part of a communication practice.

Here's another analogy. Think about an athlete training for competition; for instance, an Olympic hurdler. She doesn't just run her event over and over again and hope to get better over time. She (and her coach) take the race apart, breaking it down into its component parts. The start; the last step into the hurdle; the step over the hurdle; the step out of the hurdle; the stride length between each hurdle; the breakaway to the finish line. Each one of these skills gets perfected over hours and hours of training. And when the Olympian and her coach put the parts all back together, if the training was done well, the time should be noticeably better because the athlete will have improved her performance in a focused, logical, actionable way.

The Latimer Model

Our communication approach takes this same, skill-based, root-cause-analysis approach to speaking. Most communication coaching sees speaking as either good or bad: you either speak well, or not. But the Latimer Model takes a nonbinary approach: we see communication as a combination of four skills, each of which requires practice and preparation. And skill acquisition isn't a matter of you have it or you don't; it's a journey, as you build on your strengths and mitigate your weaknesses.

Understanding those strengths and weaknesses is a key element to our methodology. With root-cause analysis, we can pinpoint areas that need improvement and strengths to build on. By setting specific, targeted goals, the task of improvement becomes less time-intensive, less intimidating, and more easily measured over time.

In our model, we break down persuasive communication into six steps, which are then grouped into four skill areas. Underlying all of this is a pervasive practice of awareness: remaining constantly receptive to information that will enhance your understanding of yourself, your audience, and the context in which you are speaking.

The four skill areas build on each other to become a holistic, persuasive method of communication:

1. Assess: Learn to **listen** (a valuable skill often neglected in today's cacophonous world) and **analyze** the situation to better understand your audience's needs and goals and your own.

2. Message: **Collect** and **prepare** your information to be as clear, direct, and compelling as possible.
3. Document: **Create** supporting materials—a slide deck, a pre-reading document, a take-home sheet—that reinforce your message without distracting your audience.
4. Deliver: **Convey your message** with confidence and authenticity through voice, body language, and other nonverbal cues.

ASSESS   MESSAGE   DOCUMENT   DELIVER

Our goal is to break down your communication in order to build it back up. It's easy to tell someone they need to deliver a clear, comprehensive presentation. The how of it is both harder—it requires work and thoughtful preparation—and more achievable, because becoming clear and persuasive only requires focusing on a few key skills. Think of yourself as that Olympic hurdler: breaking down a complex task into measurable, improvable skills that, when practiced in isolation, will improve your overall performance.

The Four Cs of Communication

Connection: Forging a connection with our audience is the heart of persuasive communication. Convincing your audience that you care about their needs is essential to convincing them to care about whatever it is you are asking from them.

Concision: Get. To. The. Point. In the multitasking, hyper-scheduled world we live in, you have approximately ten seconds to capture your audience's attention before they move on.

Clarity: If your audience doesn't understand what you bring to them and why they are listening to you, they'll stop. Say what you need to say simply, directly, and often.

Credibility: Demonstrate your knowledge by giving your audience only the most relevant details in a way that is easy to hear and absorb. The less the audience has to work at interpreting your data, the more they'll respect you as an expert.

WHY DO YOU NEED A SYSTEM?
The High Cost of Bad Communication

Poor communication isn't just a problem in meetings and presentations (though they are the most obvious casualties). It's a problem that permeates the workplace, from meetings to phone calls, from emails to casual conversations.

Many of us want to be better communicators because we see that communicating well accomplishes goals, impresses colleagues and bosses, and creates business opportunities.

We know that being a good communicator helps make a better leader. But we don't see the other side: all the ways, in the short- and the long-term, that poor communication costs us—both individually and organizationally.

For an individual, the cost comes most prominently and insidiously as a loss of credibility. If you don't get to the point, clearly and directly, persuasively and confidently, over time your colleagues and your superiors will lose confidence in your value. And if your value decreases enough, you may find that, along with your credibility, you've lost out on opportunities to advance.

Perhaps at this point you are saying, "But I'm not in sales or marketing. Sure, I have to talk to people, but how much does persuasive communication really have to do with my job when I don't have to get anyone to buy something?" The answer, no matter what you do, is *a lot*.

A few years ago, author Daniel Pink conducted a study of more than seven thousand professionals about their responsibilities at work. He found that, across professions, 40 percent of the workday was spent on non-sales selling: trying to *persuade* someone to do something that didn't involve a purchase. It could be persuading your team to buy in on a new initiative or strategy; convincing your boss to invest in your idea or approve your budget request; influencing your colleague to approach a problem your way.

The bottom line: if you want to be seen as a leader, as an influencer, as a valuable colleague, being able to communicate effectively is essential.

And for organizations, the stakes are even higher. The leadership of our companies often fails to see how poor communication hinders the organization as a whole. Collectively, poor communication can disrupt business on a fundamental level:

1. Lack of focus: In an organization where communication is not a priority, meetings are inefficient and

ineffective. Because little gets accomplished, more meetings get scheduled, and every member of the team feels overbooked, underinformed, and generally unhappy.

2. Failure of purpose: When we are unable to communicate well on a day-to-day basis, it is generally symptomatic of a larger communication disruption. If a company can't communicate its vision and purpose, it has effectively lost both.

3. Lack of innovation: Imagine yourself in a meeting where a team is presenting a new project, product, or process. The audience has clearly tuned out: half the room is checking a device, and the other half is flipping through the PowerPoint deck to try to figure out the point of this meeting. Does anyone understand the new product or its benefits? Probably not, which means that it will likely be discarded. Multiply this across multiple meetings and multiple products, and you have a company that is stagnating.

4. Drop in morale: The sum of all these issues? The people who work and make the company successful aren't happy. And that means they aren't as productive, and/or they are looking to leave the company for a better job.

5. Loss of credibility: This can happen at both a company and an individual level. Individually, your ability to express yourself confidently and persuasively has a direct effect on your ability to effectively accomplish your goals. Company-wide, the way your goals and innovation are represented outwardly—through client meetings or public relations—has an immediate impact on your business metrics. Without clear, effective communication, everything from sales growth to stock price will decline.

So why is poor communication at an organizational level so common? In large part, it's because over the past twenty years, business communication has changed dramatically and rapidly. Years ago, it wasn't uncommon for businesses to primarily value the data aggregator—someone who could go out and pull tons of information together. The ability to dig up information was in and of itself a valuable skill. But in today's world, endless data is available to everyone, all the time. Gathering data is no longer the valuable skill; synthesizing, summarizing, and interpreting that data, however, is invaluable.

Think of when you go to the doctor. When you're sick, you don't need to know everything your doctor learned in medical school. You need to know the diagnosis, the symptoms, and the treatment. You need to know *what to do*. You want the doctor to think about who you are and why you are in the office. You need your doctor to **summarize, synthesize, and simplify what you need to know.** When you communicate in a business meeting, the same rules apply.

But evolution is hard, and not everyone has been able to keep up. Generally, I've found that most people and organizations lack a system to truly improve their communication. Instead, the focus is on creating PowerPoint templates and emphasizing "executive" (read: not nervous) demeanor. That throws the entire responsibility of communicating better on the individual, without adequately providing the tools to do so. It's a recipe for failure.

The Communication Conundrum

"According to most studies, people's number one fear is public speaking. Number two is death. Death is number two. Does that sound right? This means to the average person, if you go to a funeral, you're better off in the casket than doing the eulogy."
– Jerry Seinfeld

"There are two types of speakers: those that are nervous and those that are liars."

– Mark Twain

We all know the feeling when we stand up to speak in front of a room full of people: sweaty palms, butterflies, a rush of adrenaline so deep that our knees shake. But this personal and societal message that speaking is inherently anxiety-producing can also be a crutch—an excuse to throw up your hands and say, "I'm just a bad speaker." In fact, with practice and preparation, even the most nervous speaker can become a more confident, persuasive speaker.

Of course, our very understanding of what it means to be persuasive can hold us back, too. For many people, persuasion is just a softer word for manipulation or bullying. Persuasion isn't about finding common ground—it is about winning. It is about pushing your information across to your audience and hammering them over the head with it. But is this really accurate? I don't think so.

What if persuasion is about dialogue? What if persuasion is about creating connection? What if you, the speaker, aren't under a spotlight? What if the focus turns from "What am I going to say?" to "How are they going to react?"

Purposeful, persuasive communication requires empathy, exchange, and, perhaps most importantly, curiosity—a way of connecting your goal to the needs and wants of your audience.

When we think about persuasion as a goal-oriented, connection-focused enterprise, we can alleviate the anxiety around speaking. When we focus on moving others toward an objective through persuasive communication, we can take the emphasis off being inherently confident (in fact, sometimes the inherently confident are the worst speakers—because they think they can just stand up and wing it). Instead, success can be *made* through a step-by-step system of knowledge-gathering, analysis, message crafting, and specific delivery techniques— one that The Latimer Group has honed over years of working with major corporate clients.

Perhaps you are wondering how this type of system can fit in to your day-to-day, which is probably already overloaded with tasks. Of course, the more time you have to prepare, the better. But if you have a set of concrete steps in place, the process will be faster—and as you use it more, your speed will improve. Importantly, the concepts behind the Latimer Model are both nimble and flexible, giving you effective strategies and confidence not only in presentations and meetings, but phone calls, emails, and chance encounters in the hallway with your boss.

And, fundamentally, we all *have* to become better communicators. It isn't necessarily easy, and it isn't necessarily intuitive, but it is achievable. And we have to do it, because of the high cost of inaction. Poor communication chips away at our time, saps our morale, decreases our earnings, and ultimately disconnects us from each other, professionally and personally.

Measuring Progress

In the Latimer Model, we ask you to practice four interlocking skill areas: Assess, Message, Document, and Deliver. Along with these defined and interlocking skill areas, we've set out levels of achievement that create a pathway for individual and organizational professional growth. Rather than a "good" speaker or a "bad" speaker, we see someone with strengths and weaknesses across each of the skill areas.

At base, the difference between each of our levels is connection: how well do you connect to your audience, how much do they care about what you are telling them, and to what degree are they inspired to act by your words?

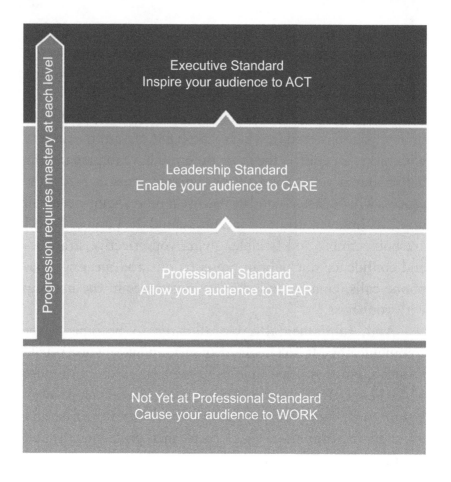

As we move through The Latimer Group curriculum, we wield precise tools aimed at cultivating that connection: clarity, brevity, impact, context, and value. We use easy-to-understand metrics to map individual abilities, provide certification for each of our levels as an individual progresses from Professional to Leadership to Executive, and create organization-wide frameworks for assessing, developing, and maintaining communication skills at all levels of need and ability.

We recognize that not everyone has to make a compelling presentation to the C-suite, and not everyone has a huge budget to defend or a big sale to close. Some people just need to motivate their direct reports or brief their colleagues. But every one of us can benefit from communicating clearly, concisely, and persuasively—and every organization can benefit from employees who feel heard, understood, and valued.

Persuasive communication is not manipulative, bullying, or one-sided. Persuasive communication is respectful, thoughtful, and a dialogue. Persuasive communication has a goal. Persuasive communication is purposeful, outcome-oriented, and opinionated. Persuasive communication can improve your speaking, boost your career, and energize your company. Persuasive communication, in short, can transform the world.

Why *Persuaded?*

Improving all our communication is the purpose of this book, and is the work that The Latimer Group, my company, has done for the past seventeen years. So how can you use the book to make your communication skills the best they can be?

First, let's be clear about what this book intends to do. This is not a book about presentation skills (though the concepts and strategies will improve any presentation). This is not a book about better meetings (though your meetings can become more effective and efficient by employing our tools).

This is a book about communicating persuasively. This is a book about forging connection with the people around you. This is a book about building credibility and creating a culture of respect. This is a book about inspiring action, building alignment, and driving good outcomes.

And, yes, it's a book about getting to the point, saving time, running better meetings, impressing the CEO, getting approval or budget or a big sale. It is a book about honing your message, building a better slide deck, and easing your nerves in front of an audience. It's a book about writing a better email, having a better phone call, running a better virtual meeting, and giving a better elevator pitch to your boss.

This book makes available to everyone the tools and techniques to systematize your communication. Here, I give you a way to examine and practice discrete skill sets, and to see the practice of clear, effective communication as cumulative and perfectible. In using this model, *anyone* can become a more powerful, persuasive speaker.

What I want you to take away is that with better communication, you can do all of it. You can communicate better with your colleagues—and have happier, shorter, more effective meetings. You can communicate better with your boss—and get better assignments, more responsibility, maybe even a promotion. You can cultivate a culture of better communication—and you can make your entire organization more efficient, more effective, more profitable. You can make your coworkers and the executive suite feel energized and inspired. That's the promise of persuasive communication.

Measuring the
Persuasion Challenge

Anjali started at her financial services company not long after she graduated from college and worked on a team that focused on recruiting new clients. She noticed that many of the ways in which the company engaged with clients were fairly traditional: quarterly reports, investor conference calls, and regular meetings with their investment advisor. She did some research and pulled together a proposal to invest in app development as a new way to service and engage with clients. Every company that Anjali interacted with had an app, and that's how she did her own banking, consumed news, and stayed in touch with friends—it seemed like a natural fit for her company. But when she gave the presentation proposing that the company roll out a suite of apps to help clients access their accounts and see investment data, her team lead refused to push it upward. "Our clients want the security and the formality of paper reports that they get in the mail," he said. "Let's focus on other ways to reach new clientele."

*

Josh was pulling together a pitch for his division's VP: to allocate resources for a new marketing push that was projected to spark an influx of new business. The initial outlay was greater than the division normally invested into marketing, but the return seemed to more than justify the cost. Josh was elated; this was a no-brainer, and his preparation for the pitch reflected his confidence in that assessment. But when he went into the meeting, the VP was uncharacteristically impatient. As soon as Josh mentioned the budget for the marketing program, she interrupted, "That's way too much! There's no way we are going to do this!" Rattled, Josh tried to keep going, but the momentum was lost. The VP left the room irritated that her time had been wasted, and Josh left frustrated that a reluctance to invest was going to lose them a great opportunity.

What happened? In both these scenarios, the speaker lost sight of his or her *audience:* how the persuasive goal would appear to them, how much change it would entail for them, and what sort of effort or investment it required from them. Anjali and Josh allowed their own enthusiasm to cloud their understanding, or effort to understand, the potential reactions of the audience. And in both cases, because the speakers ignored this critical element of their preparation, their message lacked a critical building block for success.

A FOUNDATION FOR SUCCESS

If you set out to build a house, the first thing you do is make sure that you put down a solid foundation. Otherwise, the walls will be shaky, the floor will slope, and your roof might cave in. The foundation makes the rest of the building strong and secure.

The same is true in persuasive communication. Many people begin their preparation for the big meeting or the big presentation with a flawed first step. Many people go straight into patching together a slide deck, or simply laying out their main points. But the most effective and persuasive speakers take the time to lay a foundation before they start building their arguments. In communication, that means cultivating an audience-oriented mindset that sets out to understand their perspective—their potential reactions, concerns, and the elements that may give the conversation a high degree of difficulty.

Many of us, when we think about preparing for a speech or a presentation, think about information gathering. We think about what materials make us look like experts, proficient in our field, and adept at solving problems. If we really put some time into it, we think about how to best organize this information to create an impact or have a logical flow.

But focusing on the *what* and *how* is premature. To successfully and powerfully *persuade* an audience, we need to think about *why* (an idea brilliantly captured by Simon Sinek; see sidebar). What is our goal, and how does it affect our audience? What does our audience care about and need from us? What are we asking from them, and how easy or painful will it be for our audience to say yes? Remember, our goal is to move away from the messenger mindset—in which we care only about delivering information, and don't consider what the receiver might feel or think of it—and toward purposeful, persuasive communication.

Harnessing the Power of Why

Simon Sinek, author and motivational speaker, has identified a powerful way to think about expressing ourselves and connecting with others. He notes that most people are able to describe *what* they do; some can tell us *how* they do it. But a small few can articulate *why* they do something—the purpose or belief that drives their action. Sinek uses Apple as an example:

> If Apple were like everyone else, a marketing message from them might sound like this: "We make great computers. They're beautifully designed, simple to use and user friendly. Want to buy one?" "Meh." That's how most of us communicate. That's how most marketing and sales are done, that's how we communicate interpersonally. We say what we do, we say how we're different or better and we

expect some sort of a behavior, a purchase, a vote, something like that ... But it's uninspiring. Here's how Apple actually communicates. "Everything we do, we believe in challenging the status quo. We believe in thinking differently. The way we challenge the status quo is by making our products beautifully designed, simple to use and user friendly. We just happen to make great computers. Want to buy one?" Totally different, right? You're ready to buy a computer from me. I just reversed the order of the information. What it proves to us is that people don't buy what you do; people buy why you do it.

The ability to communicate your *why* is incredibly powerful and inspirational; if you are able to harness the *why* of your goal, you will have an immediate advantage when it comes to communication.

At this point, you might be thinking, *When I have to pull together a presentation or a speech in just a few days or even hours, how can I stop and contemplate my goals and my audience's perspective? At this rate, I won't even have a slide deck done in time!*

I get it. Everyone is short on time. When you are already hard-pressed to pull together a basic outline, pausing to assess can feel like a luxury. But if you are tempted to skip this step (or this chapter)—*don't.*

Think about it this way: investing ten minutes into preparation before you make an outline or put together your first slide will save you time gathering irrelevant material, earn you the respect and goodwill of your audience, and return a much greater likelihood of success (which will also earn compound interest in the form of greater credibility in future interactions). That seems like a pretty good deal.

If you do not know precisely what action you want your audience to take the moment you walk *out* of the room, then you are not ready to walk *into* the room.

To Anjali, moving toward an app-based method of client communication felt natural. It didn't seem like a big deal to roll it out widely. When she debriefed with an older colleague, she complained that Todd, her team leader, had dismissed it so summarily. Her colleague told her, "You have to realize that he's been here for thirty years. Client communication has always been done in a particular way—I don't think they've substantially changed it the entire time he's been here. This is a huge shift for him." Anjali realized that what felt like a small shift to her appeared like a seismic change to Todd. A few days later, she brought in some new research to Todd about the appeal of apps in financial services and suggested that they test out this approach with a limited number of clients. The proposal now felt like dipping a toe into the water, rather than diving in headfirst. Todd agreed to take it up to the head of investor relations.

*

In his enthusiasm for his proposal, Josh had forgotten to think about what he was asking of the VP, and what the proposal might require of her. In his postmortem, Josh started asking around for more information about the VP and what was happening in her office. It turned out that she was part of the transition team for a major new acquisition, and things weren't going well. Merging the new company into already existing resources had created myriad budget pressures, and the VP was under a great deal of stress. In this atmosphere, any new budget request was going to be tricky. If Josh had known this ahead of time, his message would have been entirely different.

Observing the Field of Play

Both Josh and Anjali realized that they hadn't really understood the degree of difficulty their persuasive goal represented. This is the Persuasion Challenge: **understanding the amount of change you are asking from your audience, and the level of involvement or investment they'll need to put in.** Your Persuasion Challenge may have other variables as well, but these two variables are always going to be present, and your success often hinges on how well you understand them.

In purposeful communication, the first step will always be to understand if the opportunity in front of you will be an easy one (little involvement required from your audience, and little or no change) or a difficult one (a large budget ask or significant involvement, and major change required). Understanding where your goal lands in this field of play will determine a great deal of how you approach your topic.

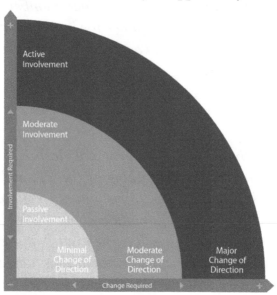

The key here is to remember to approach this from the *audience* perspective. What tangible thing are you asking them to provide (time, money, head count)? What is the degree of change you are asking of them? What may seem like an insignificant or easy request to you may be, at that time and in the audience's context, a much more challenging ask. I will get into more detail in later chapters about knowing your audience. For now, the key is to try to adopt your audience's perspective, and to arm yourself with some basic knowledge of the context in which they are operating.

UNDERSTANDING THE AXES

The X-Axis: Level of Change

It is human nature to resist change.

How often have you heard that? On some level, the prevalence of this sentiment can be attributed to its truth; you can see it in your own behavior. Do you choose the same cereal for breakfast? Do you have a routine stop for coffee on your way to work? Do you go on vacation to the same resort every year? Familiarity breeds comfort, while change can feel threatening.

But the truthfulness of the sentiment also depends a great deal on context. Think about technology, for instance. Let's say that Sam has an iPhone and has upgraded from version to version a few times over the past few years. If he is offered the latest model, he'll be happy to take it—even if it means having to update all his apps, learn a new operating system, and get used to changes in hardware. Even with that degree of change, it's a process Sam is comfortable with. But Sam's dad has always used a flip phone. If someone asks him to move to the latest iPhone, making that change will be much harder. He'll have to learn to use an entirely new interface and adapt to new ways of using the phone.

Some people crave change, while others are wary of the risks. The same change might require a greater leap for one person than another. With this in mind, the first variable to assess as you begin to plan your communication is the *level of change* your proposal requires—not only in general, but also for your specific audience.

The more change you are recommending (change of plan, direction, strategy, brand, etc.), the more difficult the challenge. By correctly assessing the level of change necessary, you can be prepared with a persuasive message that comprehends and addresses the significance of the change—and anticipates skeptical, even aggressive interrogation. Building in responses to the most likely questions can defuse some of this tension; in addition, you'll be prepared to respond sympathetically, respectfully, and thoroughly to objections.

The Y-Axis: Level of Involvement

Have you ever been interrupted during a presentation by the question, "Okay, but what do you need from me?" If so, it's not surprising—the level of involvement is often the most pressing concern on an audience's mind. Consider the difference between asking someone for approval to accelerate the timeline for a new initiative, and asking someone to give approval, fund an expanded budget, and hire two new employees to accelerate the timeline. The level of involvement will impact how your audience views any change, big or small.

Will the idea simply require audience approval, a low level of involvement, or will the audience need to take some risks and commit resources? Is this particular audience lending support and approval for your recommendation? Will they have to implement some of the changes, or manage those that will? Or are you asking for a commitment of resources, time, and risk? The more you ask of the audience, the more they need to believe in you and your message.

Having a sense of context doesn't mean you need to do a background check or do a deep dive into the business practices of your audience. A quick Google search, looking at the company stock price over the past six months, or asking a few questions of colleagues or reports can give you a quick idea of what's at stake.

Questions to Ask

When you are determining the level of change or involvement, some basic questions can help guide your assessment.

Level of Change

- Does this request involve a change of strategy?
- Does this idea promote a new product or service?
- Is this a divergence from the existing brand?
- Does the request fit within your current line of work?
- Does the idea align with your organizational mission?
- Is this concept designed to appeal to your existing clientele?
- Do you anticipate selling this concept to a market outside of your current one?
- Does the change launch an innovative new direction for your organization?
- Will this request capitalize on the current successes of your business?
- Does this change the way you'll do business?

Level of Involvement

- Does this initiative require additional financial resources?
- Will you require more staff to take on the challenge?
- Do you have the capacity to take on the new initiative within your current team?
- Does your current team have the skill set to launch this new program?
- Will you need to cut other planned projects to fit this into the budget?
- Will you need to invest significantly to get this off the ground?
- Will the outcome of other projects be dependent on the success of this one?
- Will you have to divert talent from other projects to take this on?
- Do you have to reallocate budget to accommodate this request?
- Are you requesting support for this initiative without additional resources?

CULTIVATING AWARENESS

When we look at a Persuasion Challenge, one fundamental skill helps us understand how to approach a conversation in a way that bolsters our chances for success. That skill is awareness: of ourselves, of the context, of our audience, and of our own message. When we practice the art of awareness, every other element of communication becomes enriched.

Self-Awareness

Think about your own strengths and weaknesses, and ask yourself some questions: how do I interact with others? Do I ask questions? Do I listen? Do I tend to interrupt? Do I project confidence and credibility? When we are aware of our weaknesses—a tendency to equivocate, a lack of active listening skills—we can find ways to compensate or eliminate them; when we know our strengths—genuine curiosity, strong expertise—we can build on them. And once we have an idea how other people perceive us, we can start to think about how we can leverage that perception into a connection.

Self-awareness is a big component of Emotional Intelligence—an understanding of one's own emotions and how those emotions impact the people around one. Be aware of the energy you are emitting, because the people you work with certainly are aware of it. I'm not asking you to stifle your emotions. Rather, be conscious of how you might project your own anger, happiness, frustration, or fear, and take steps to mitigate the effects of these emotions on your audience.

Situational Awareness

The key to being situationally aware is to remember it is not the same as audience awareness. You might know your audience very well and have a great sense of their process and what questions they tend to ask. But if their situation has changed—maybe they have a new boss, or they've lost a big client, or they face a merger—that process and those questions may change. They may not be as receptive to a new idea. Offering approval without risking resources might typically be a low level of involvement—unless the approver has suffered setbacks recently and feels that her reputation is vulnerable. Your reasonable budget might sound wildly expensive to a unit leader who just had to invest deeply elsewhere; likewise, a request for some staff hours might be onerous for the VP who just had to lay off 10 percent of the division. Take stock of your audience's environment so that you can anticipate their state of mind.

Audience Awareness

With all the research tools at our fingertips, this might be the area in which a lack of awareness is most baffling. Use LinkedIn or other networking sites to do your research—how long has your client been at his company? How long has she worked in the industry? What school did he go to, and what was his degree in? Did she serve in the military?

Let's be clear—this isn't profiling. None of this information should lead to firm conclusions. But it can open doors of discovery. If someone has a degree in accounting, I can guess that we'll spend our first few minutes together talking about business case. If another person has worked for thirty years in marketing, I know she'll be drawn toward our marketing plan. These kinds of soft assumptions give us a place to start building a connection. That doesn't mean that you exclude marketing from your proposal to an accounting client or eliminate the business case when you approach a client with a marketing background. But it does give you a chance to craft a narrative that speaks to their interests and experience. I'll get into the specifics of audience awareness and how to know more about your audience in later chapters.

Message Awareness

Once we understand ourselves, our audience, and our mutual environment, finding an effective message comes more naturally. Our questions become: what is my key message? Is it simple and memorable? Do my key points speak to my audience? Do they address my audience's concerns and pressures? For this day and this audience, is my goal achievable? The answers to these questions form the spine of any persuasive communication. I'll address how to use these elements to craft a powerful message in coming chapters.

Two Ways to Deal with a Difficult Situation

Cultivating awareness isn't just a state of mind: it's an active, deliberate way to give yourself a base of knowledge with which to approach any communication. More specifically, understanding the scope of your Persuasion Challenge—especially when you realize that you are facing a particularly tough challenge—allows you to:

1. Dedicate more time to preparing for your communication. Put an extra thirty minutes or an hour on your calendar specifically to concentrate on a particularly difficult challenge.
2. Ask for help—whether in background information, credibility adding, or relationship building. If my colleague knows the person I'm going to meet, I might ask her for tips, ask her to put in a positive word for me, or even invite her to attend the meeting.

CASE STUDY: Sophia and Miguel

Using the Persuasion Challenge framework to understand your audience

Sophia's team had been asked to solve an urgent issue: customers were unhappy with the service they were getting and weren't hesitating to broadcast their feelings all over the Web.

The solution Sophia's group had come up with was to move from relying 100 percent on voice support to text support first.

The team had spent two months on intense research and rehearsed the presentation to perfection. Everyone knew his or her role, and when they walked into the conference room to present to Miguel, their boss, they were excited, confident, and eager to get their 'yes' and move on to implementation.

But as they progressed through the slide deck, Sophia immediately noticed that Miguel had a skeptical look on his face. He thumbed quickly through her deck, racing ahead of her presentation.

Finally, he held one finger in the air, interrupting her in mid-sentence. With a raised eyebrow, he began a deluge of questions. He challenged their solution, parsed every detail in the data, and positioned himself firmly against the concept.

As the team leader, Sophia struggled to maintain her composure and keep the confident, upbeat tone that she intended to carry throughout the meeting. She was genuinely caught off guard; she hadn't anticipated this line of questioning.

Finally, wanting to keep the door open, she moved to wrap up the meeting without getting a firm 'no.' So she simply said, "Miguel, I can see we've got a lot of work to do here. Let my team regroup on this and come back in a way that's responsive to your concerns."

With the team back in her office, they ran through what had gone wrong.

Sophia asked her colleagues, "Was what we were asking for clear enough?"

The team was smart and able to be self-critical. It was clear to them that they had made their case: a shift from voice to text support. And they had the data to show that was what their customers wanted as well. Additionally, they had taken a close look at the budget considerations to be able to make the transition.

A member of Sophia's team, Lu, spoke up. "Maybe what we were asking for made sense to us and might even have made sense to Miguel. But maybe we were asking too much for him."

What happened?

In Sophia's case, she had clearly thought through what she wanted. She planned her entire presentation around the research she and her team had compiled. She built her argument around the goal of implementing a new, technologically advanced, customer communications system. She had a compelling story and a clear explanation of the benefits to the organization. She knew her audience and had experience appealing to them for other initiatives, so she felt prepared and ready to present.

But Sophia had not understood the significance of the change she was seeking. In her mind, the business case was a no-brainer. They could eliminate costly and annoying hold times, initial troubleshooting could be done more quickly, and customers would have a transcript of their interaction to refer back to if they had questions or if the problem cropped up again. But from Miguel's perspective, the change would call for a radical transformation in the way the company did business.

If Sophia had imagined why Miguel might be resistant to her proposed change, she might have considered:

> **Added distance in the customer relationship:** Miguel feared that his company would lose the personal touch with the customer, and therefore lose the valuable feedback that customers often provided.
>
> **Unknown runaway costs:** Miguel was concerned about which unknown or unanticipated costs might embarrass him when they tried to implement the new technology. And if the program didn't work well,

costs would soar again if they had to switch back to the old system.

Fear of retraining workers: Miguel worried about the shift in responsibilities for the customer service reps as they moved from high-touch voice support to the faster but more impersonal text system.

What should Sophia do?

Sophia needed better tools to help her assess just how difficult the Persuasion Challenge was for her team. She needed to answer the two big questions:

1. How much change is being proposed?
2. What degree of involvement will be required from the audience to execute that change?

Asking specific, targeted questions for each of these areas (see sidebar on page 23) would allow Sophia's team to fully comprehend the issue from their audience's point of view. As a team, they would put themselves in Miguel's shoes and begin to understand the magnitude of the change he was facing. Once they understood what they were asking of him, they'd be much better equipped to prepare for the meeting effectively.

In evaluating their request with the Persuasion Challenge Questionnaire, the team recognized that their proposal required significant involvement and the highest degree of change:

Level of Change: One of Miguel's fears was "added distance in the customer relationship." This initiative would radically change the way the company interacted with its customers. By implementing a text-message system, they would revolutionize the way they do business and it would change the customer experience. Sophia was asking for a High Degree of Change.

Level of Involvement: The new text message initiative would require a significant commitment. The company would need to dedicate resources to developing the technology. They'd need to train the employees on new protocol. They'd need to invest in a communication campaign with their customers to unveil the new process. Miguel was worried about "runaway costs" and was "afraid of retraining workers." The acknowledgment of risk would be crucial to their success. This initiative would require a Significant Degree of Involvement.

Sophia and her team needed to demonstrate that these challenges would be mitigated by the upside potential of the new program. The many efficiencies created with this program and the process improvements could significantly enhance the customer experience and lead to more customers. They also needed to acknowledge the change and Miguel's concerns.

The team reassembled in a conference room the next week. As people were taking their seats around the table, a slide show scrolled through images of the evolution of communication. They saw an antique candlestick phone, a rotary phone, the first cordless phones, and early mobile phones. A tangle of wires showed a primitive switchboard. There were images of messengers delivering telegraphs, newsboys selling the evening paper, fax machines spitting out messages. The montage sped up as it moved to current communication trends like Twitter, Snapchat, and instant messaging.

"Fear, resistance, disbelief..." Sophia began. "These are some of the emotions people felt as they first were asked to accept these new methods of communication. But over time, society has embraced these changes and businesses which remain relevant have too." She handed the presentation over to her team, who gracefully acknowledged the degree of change they were requesting, and carefully addressed the concerns Miguel had raised in the previous meeting. As they built their case, they reinforced the business rationale behind their recommendation, while remaining sensitive to the degree of change necessary to implement the initiative.

Miguel's body language was different this time around. He jotted notes, nodded at times, and made eye contact with his direct reports around the table. When the team wrapped up the presentation without having been interrupted, they were eager to open it up for questions.

Armed with an extraordinary amount of data from customer and employee research, the team was prepared for the following hour of tough questioning. Miguel still had his concerns about the customer connection, budget overruns, and employee training, but he was open to the concept. By revealing the vulnerabilities and recognizing his concerns with the change, the team was able to put Miguel in a place to listen and be open to new ideas. The Persuasion Challenge created context and provided Sophia's team with the framework they needed to get the required permission from Miguel to go ahead with the plan to introduce text messaging into their customer communication program. It took more than thorough research and detailed data and spreadsheets. It took the acknowledgment of the change and involvement required. The team needed to respect Miguel and make a direct connection with him in order to be successful.

*

Remember, the Persuasion Challenge acts as your communication foundation. With a solid understanding of the impact your communication will have on your audience, you can begin to build a strong and persuasive argument that won't fall apart with the first question or criticism. You can move on to the next step—Assess—with confidence that you understand the challenge in front of you.

Consider the Context

Your ability to speak well and be persuasive begins long before you open your mouth.

Assess—the first skill in the Latimer Model—lays the foundation for everything that comes next. Without assessing your audience, your message, your own credibility, and your context, you are much more likely to speak in a way that is unconvincing, uninspiring, and counterproductive. If you take the time to assess thoroughly, every step that follows will be easier, quicker, and more effective.

Conventional communications coaching might focus on your slide deck, or what you do with your hands, or how nervous you look. But those are just tools for the real purpose and power of communication: connection. Great communication requires connection between the speaker and the audience—and that requires listening and analysis. The good news is that we are all capable of connection, and with some investment of time and commitment, the payoff can be significant.

Connection is built both inwardly and outwardly, by knowing ourselves and knowing our audience. The Latimer Model reflects this by dividing the assessment stage into listening and analyzing. In Listen, you assess outwardly, as you understand the audience and what they care about; Analyze focuses inward, assessing your own strengths and weaknesses.

This two-step process reframes your perspective from "What do I need to say" to "What does *my audience* need to hear?"; allows you to focus on areas of weakness (Do I need to learn more about my audience? Sharpen my message? Find ways to build credibility?); and gives you a foundation of knowledge on which to build in every other step of the Latimer Model. (For a checklist to guide you through these skills, please see the appendix: "Assess Effectiveness Review.")

Deborah was an office manager at a company that had a corporate culture of branded giveaways for employees and clients: hats, mugs, shirts, even medals. She came to a workshop with a presentation that had totally flopped, and she wasn't sure why. In it, she outlined an inventory she'd overseen of all the giveaway materials they kept on-site. She'd discovered that they had multiple storage sites, hundreds of items that were going unused, and several thousand square feet was being taken up for storage. Meantime, a period of hiring and growth had resulted in a cramped workspace for employees.

In her presentation, Deborah proposed streamlining the ordering process for giveaways. Rather than keeping items on hand, she wanted to get rid of all the stale inventory and convert ordering to an online, on-demand process. Storage space could then be converted to office space, and the company would save money by ordering only the items that would be used.

As we talked through the negative reaction to her proposal, I asked Deborah to go back and really listen to the objections her audience had. After a few conversations with her colleagues, she reported back: for many longtime employees, the culture of having giveaways on hand, immediately available to see, to grab whenever they needed it, felt important. They looked forward to the experience of going to a storage room to pull out a mug or a shirt for their client. Further, many of the items felt sentimentally significant to them, and the thought of off-loading them to make space felt painful.

With this information, Deborah was able to reorient her message to acknowledge the company's concerns and find a compromise that respected their objections while moving toward a solution for their space constraints. By adding a specific, conscious step of listening, *Deborah was able to speak more clearly to her audience.*

STEP ONE: LISTEN

The best communicators are strong listeners. Few people focus on listening as a skill, but without it, every other step in creating persuasive communication becomes much more difficult. To create connection, you need to know what is important to people and ally what you need with their priorities. But it will be pretty hard to figure out people's priorities and connect with them if you don't listen.

The best listeners tune out the ambient noise, turn off the distractions and show respect for the person speaking. They quiet their inner monologue and really pay attention to what is being said.

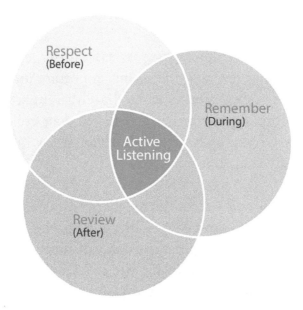

Remember, listening is not a passive activity. It's not just letting someone else talk while you figure out what you are going to say next. The passive act of receiving sound waves is called "hearing." Listening, on the other hand, is an active, engaged mode, in which you focus on comprehending and remembering what you are hearing.

The Latimer Group breaks this down into the "3Rs of Active Listening":

Respect: Before you start the meeting or take the call, eliminate all possible distractions. Shut your laptop. Mute your cell phone. Close your email. Respect the opportunity you have before you to truly listen.

Remember: Before and during the meeting or call, use techniques to help retain information as it is delivered. Prepare by reviewing any previous conversations you've had, think about the goal of the conversation, and write down a few questions. During the conversation, take good notes. Start a dialogue during the meeting so that you are engaged and more likely to retain the information. Ask a question for clarification.

Review: After the meeting or call is over, spend a few minutes reviewing decisions, important information, and next steps. Immediately reiterating this information, whether verbally to your colleagues or by writing up a synopsis for yourself, will help keep it fresh in your mind.

Listening can be considered both an assessment tool (a way to get to know your audience and plan a message) and a delivery technique that can cultivate greater connection with your audience (by allowing you to adapt and respond to information you learn in the midst of your communication).

Using listening in the second way will come up again in later chapters, but the skills of *active listening* are fundamentally the same, whether you are deploying them while researching, in a pre-meeting phone call, or during the meeting itself.

Active listening techniques help you both listen better and let your audience *know* that you are listening to them (which may compel them to tell you more, since they know they are being heard). Be active, engaged, and responsive.

Ask questions: Cultivate genuine curiosity. When you are curious about your audience, you'll ask interesting questions that they'll want to answer. Listen to what they have to say and ask another question about that. Of course, this won't be an infinite process, but you might be amazed at where one incisive question and one or two follow-up questions will take you.

Use body language: If you are meeting in person, make sure that you communicate your active listening with the right body language. Keep up eye contact, try not to cross your arms, and don't look around the room or over the speaker's shoulder. Definitely don't look at your phone! Ideally, any devices will be turned off, so that you aren't distracted by ringing or buzzing.

Take notes: When you write something down, you signal that you consider it important enough to remember. And you remember it! Notes can be invaluable when you have a follow-up meeting and want to be able to refer back to specific numbers or other details.

Accept dissent: A big part of listening is giving up control. Once you turn over the floor, you need to be able to accept that the other person may have a completely different perspective than you do. You might have fundamental disagreements. But by listening well, you might find some common ground. At the very least, you'll show that you can treat other viewpoints with respect and empathy.

React: If you are in the middle of a presentation, be prepared to adjust what you are going to say to what you are hearing. You won't always be able to eliminate information, but you can acknowledge the hurdles that you've just learned about. The more comfortable and confident you are with your message, the more easily you'll be able to adjust on the fly.

When you master the art of listening, the information you receive will help you polish a message that feels personal, well-crafted, and persuasive. You'll forge a connection with your audience, which will make them feel comfortable with you and more receptive to your ideas now and in the future. And you'll become known as someone who listens well and respects their audience.

3-D Listening

We all know that when we talk about dimensions, there's a hierarchy at play. One-dimensional is flat and not very exciting, i.e., *superficial.* Two-dimensional offers a little more information, but it *lacks depth.* Three-dimensional, on the other hand, is nuanced and complex, *realistic and complete.*

The same terminology can describe the way we listen. Not all listening is of equal quality or value (though of course, it is better than not listening at all, which is what the vast majority of people do in a business setting).

One-dimensional listening: You pay attention, take notes, hear the words I'm saying, and can repeat back the content. You've listened at a surface level and have retained the information—but not more than that.

Two-dimensional listening: You understand the implication of my words beyond the literal meaning, because you know something about me, my company, my industry, or my situation. This awareness means that you can connect what I'm saying to a bigger picture, and have a wider view of my words and the intent behind those words.

Three-dimensional listening: You hear my words, notice the implication of my nonverbal communication, and notice what I'm leaving out. You take in facial expressions, changes in tone, body language, and eye contact. In other words, you listen to *what* I say, *how* I say it, and what I *don't* say.

Now, much of the time we don't even listen in one dimension: the distractions of our modern workplace mean that we actually retain only a fraction of what we hear in a communication setting. But when we can push ourselves to listen beyond a single dimension, and take in two or even three dimensions, we tap into a much fuller range of knowledge. When we understand this difference, we can prepare ourselves to listen more deeply; we can prepare to hear the words behind the words, and to see the information that's being shared without words.

Create a Listening Plan

When we go into a meeting, we all usually have some sort of plan for what we want to say. But how many of us make a listening plan?

Now, listening may seem like the simplest thing in the world to do, and the idea of taking a few minutes to craft a plan for doing so might seem unnecessary. But most of us, no matter how well-intentioned, are actually terrible listeners. We live in a hyper-paced, multitasking, information-overloaded business world. Even when we think we are listening, we usually only have about 50 percent of our brain—if that—tuned to the person speaking. More likely, you are thinking about: what you want to say next; the next meeting; that email you need to write to your boss; the angry client you need to appease; your kid's doctor appointment; where you put the handout you need for tomorrow's big presentation; lunch; the budget overrun you need to justify.

The beauty of a listening plan is that it gives your listening intention, structure, and purpose. By taking just a few minutes to outline what's important to hear and what you want to achieve by listening, you'll have new motivation to pay attention, take notes, and really absorb the information you are receiving.

What goes into a listening plan? First, think about your goal—both your short-term goal, what you want out of this specific meeting, and your long-term goal, what you want in the next meeting, the next quarter, or even over the next year. Then, think about the following:

- What don't you know that could help you achieve your goals?
- What goals do the other people have?
- What pressures are they facing?
- What do they think about you, your product, your company, or your initiative?
- How does your goal impact their business?
- How big of an ask are you making of them? Remember, what may seem like a small ask to you might actually be a significant ask to them—that's something you are trying to find out.

Make a determined effort to hear all this information in what they say. Plan out some questions that will help elicit this information. Take notes, so that you don't ask them to repeat something they've already told you.

Another benefit of staying focused as part of a listening plan is that it makes it more likely that you'll pick up on your audience's nonverbal communication. Pay attention to changes in body language, tone of voice, or facial expressions. Most people instinctively react in these nonverbal ways to information that they feel strongly about, either negatively or positively. If you mention prices and your audience starts taking copious notes, you can infer that cost is important to them. If you talk about building community and the CEO in the room leans forward to listen more intently, that's a selling point.

A listening plan can give you an advantage in any situation. If you are going into a meeting as a team, it has the added benefit of making sure that the entire team is aligned on goals and focused on the same key information. You can also divide and conquer—if each person on the team is listening for particular information, or focused in on one particular person, you have a better chance of capturing a wider range of information.

If you need more convincing of the power of a listening plan, consider the fact that it's a strategy used by the FBI in high-stakes situations, such as hostage negotiations. In *Never Split the Difference*, Chris Voss, a former FBI agent, notes, "In some standoffs, we had as many as five people on the line, analyzing the information as it came in, offering behind-the-scenes input and guidance." He goes on to explain why they use this strategy: "It's really not that easy to listen well. We are easily distracted. We engage in selective listening, hearing only what we want to hear, our minds acting on a cognitive bias for consistency rather than truth."

When we go into a meeting with a prospective client, the Latimer Group team talks about our message plan and our slide deck. But we also come up with a listening plan: what are we trying to learn? What don't we know? What should we ask, and what are we listening for in the answers? We discuss who we know in the room, what we know about them, and what we are most interested in finding out. If there's more than one of us going into the meeting, we might divide up responsibility: each one of us will watch for a reaction to specific items. Afterward, we can compare our observations: When we mentioned time investment, the head of HR crossed her arms; when we talked about impact, we saw a lot of heads nodding. By making a plan ahead of time, we focus more in the moment and retain more information to analyze later.

With a listening plan, focus and retention skyrocket. Not only will you learn more, but your audience will feel your intention and attention, which will build your credibility and create a strong relationship. It's a simple step that can pay off dramatically.

STEP TWO: ANALYZE

When we fail to communicate powerfully, it typically comes down to one (or more) of the following: we didn't know our audience, our message was disorganized, our audience didn't believe in us. This second step, Analyze, allows us to identify *our own* areas of weakness and work to address them *before* we communicate.

This analysis typically reveals that we need to work a little bit on each area—and that can be helpful information. But this tool becomes invaluable when we realize that we have one or two areas of glaring weakness—areas of vulnerability that would otherwise only become apparent when we fail to achieve our objective.

To help The Latimer Group in this analysis, we've developed a metaphor for successful communication: the Leverage Mindset. In the same way that you can use leverage to lift heavy objects—much heavier than you could typically pick up on your own—you can use leverage to move your audience to action. But to build an effective lever, you have to be able to honestly and accurately assess all the elements that affect its power.

In this metaphor, an understanding of the audience is the fulcrum; the message is the lever; and credibility is the force exerted at the end of the lever. Do you know your audience well enough? If not, try to learn more so you can move the fulcrum. Is your message simple and clear and valuable enough? If not, work on distilling your message more powerfully, which will lengthen your lever. And do you have enough credibility? If not, focus on building more.

To prepare a persuasive argument we must assess how to increase leverage. The Leverage Mindset is a communication tool that will help you get into the mindset of persuasive communication.

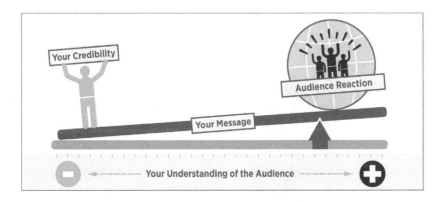

The Fulcrum: How Well You Understand Your Audience

My coaching client, Kwame, was in charge of a major training initiative across a five-hundred-person division at his company. He was a little more than halfway through implementation when the VP of the division asked for a status report. Kwame did his homework. He asked around about what this VP cared about the most. He consistently heard that the VP was more interested in the experiential than the quantifiable. Kwame also knew, from quizzing a few people who worked with the VP, that he was already really excited by what Kwame was doing, and eager to hear stories about specific employee experiences. So while Kwame pulled together a few illustrative metrics, he mostly focused on the anecdotal to show what progress the division had made. This was a huge project for Kwame, and he spent a lot of time preparing to make the case that his training was having a significant impact on these employees.

But when the day came to make the presentation, the VP was called into a last-minute meeting and wasn't available. His second-in-command, Sarah, met Kwame instead. So his tailored presentation was no longer going to be given to the person it was tailored for, and what he'd prepared was a very poor fit for his new audience. Kwame had never even heard Sarah's name before and knew zero about her. Later, he learned that this executive was extremely data-oriented, was already skeptical about the work Kwame was doing, and had no interest in anecdotal evidence.

Kwame figured all of this out pretty quickly after spending a few minutes in the room with her. Sarah was clearly unimpressed with Kwame's work, feeling that what he was doing was a waste of time, resources, and money, and all the stories he'd carefully prepared made no impression on her whatsoever. She obviously felt that Kwame was trying to hide his program's ineffectiveness under the cover of anecdotal evidence, rather than offering up hard, data-backed evidence of its impact. And she wasn't afraid to tell Kwame just that, as bluntly and brusquely as she could. As she took him to task, all the people who'd been so helpful about intel on the VP averted their eyes—no one was going to leap to Kwame's defense or give him any cover. By the time that Kwame realized he was woefully unprepared, it was too late.

What went wrong? Kwame had spent time researching, prepping, and organizing his presentation to directly meet the needs of his audience. But what he didn't do was think about who else might be in the room, what she might need or want, and who would be the primary audience if the VP was not in the room. Kwame needed to have the flexibility and the agility to make his message resonate not just with one person, but many. He needed to push his assessment: to both listen and analyze the potential situation and the likely response to his communication.

The fundamental purpose of all communication is to create connection. And in order to create connection, it is crucial to understand your audience. This understanding permeates the Latimer Model. I'll talk about the audience again in the next chapter, which addresses Message, and in chapter 7, which looks at an audience's unique perspectives and how they can shape the way we connect with them.

Here, though, your understanding of the audience serves a specific purpose. In the Leverage Mindset, audience awareness acts as the fulcrum of your communication, and where it sits helps determine how long your lever (your message) needs to be and how much force (your credibility) you need to exert in order to lift (inspire, motivate, cause to act) your audience. Understanding where your leverage is weak or strong can help you put in the work to give your communication effort the best chance at success.

In this portion of your analysis, consider the following questions. How fully you can answer them will show you where your fulcrum sits and will help you determine whether you need to do more to move it.

1. Who is my audience?
2. What is their background and history?
3. What is their point of view?
4. What will be valuable to them?

The Lever: The Message

I'd been working with Priscilla for years, and she'd recently moved to an executive position in a new company. She told me she'd like The Latimer Group to be involved with her new team but needed some time to get settled.

A few months later, she called me in to meet her managing directors, who would decide whether or not to bring The Latimer Group in for training with their groups.

As I prepared for the meeting, I thought about the Leverage Mindset. In assessing my strengths and weaknesses, I thought that delivering The Latimer Group message would be a strength, but that my potential weakness was in my knowledge of the audience, because I had had limited interaction with the MDs, and in my credibility, because I feared I would be perceived only as an ally of Priscilla's.

I focused on bolstering my knowledge of the MDs by talking several times with Priscilla about what she perceived as their skills, their needs, and their backgrounds; not only did I listen carefully to the information she was giving me, but I paid attention to her tone and vocabulary as she spoke. Was she positive, or was she complaining about them? Did she seem excited by their role in the company, or frustrated?

I also asked Priscilla specifically about whether our long-standing business relationship would be an asset or a liability. She told me that she was concerned that they might feel like she was forcing them into this meeting and toward the training.

Based on my information gathering, I realized I needed to work on my message. I needed to make sure that my message was inclusive, put their needs first, and felt like a collaboration rather than a hard sell. I started the meeting with a series of questions about the MDs' role in the organization and their goals. Through their answers, I quickly discovered that they recognized a need for our training, and that if my association with Priscilla was a weakness, it wasn't a deal-breaker.

Once I'd established this connection with my audience, I could launch into my strong message about the advantages and benefits of our work, both on an individual level and an organizational one. By analyzing my potential strengths and weaknesses, I was able to adjust my message to better suit my audience.

Another set of questions can help you analyze the effectiveness of your message. Again, I'll talk more about honing and strengthening your message in the next chapter. For now, we're trying to understand our strengths and weaknesses so that we can use our preparation time most effectively and efficiently.

As you think about your message, ask yourself:

1. What is my key message?
2. Is it clear and simple?
3. Is it relevant to the audience?
4. Is it memorable?
5. Is it valuable?
6. Are the benefits and costs quantified?
7. Are the risks of not moving forward made clear?
8. Is the level of detail correct?
9. Is there a clear call-to-action, followed by next steps?

The Force: Your Credibility

Steve was working as a consultant for a major international conglomerate that had offices all over the world. His contact there, Michiko, was someone he'd met in his previous job, and when Michiko moved to the conglomerate, she brought Steve on board. Michiko was a great executive: smart, good at her job, and highly respected. She was an American but lived in

London and ran the Singapore and Australian offices. When Steve first began traveling to Singapore, Brisbane, and Perth to work with employees of the conglomerate, he made sure to let people know he was there because of his strong professional relationship with Michiko. Steve knew Michiko's reputation in the company, and he figured that while he was an unknown, invoking Michiko's name would pass on some credibility that he could then build on by his own merits—not a bad strategy.

Except that Steve hadn't read the room right. Rather than conferring credibility, referencing Michiko made some people more *skeptical, and made them think that Steve had* less *credibility and that he was being flown in from America just because he was Michiko's friend, not because he was the best person for the job. Steve had to quickly adjust, and from then on, while he didn't hide his connection to Michiko, he made sure that he emphasized that the connection didn't make any difference to anyone in the room. Instead, Steve shifted the focus to what qualified him as a consultant.*

Chances are, you've never really spent much time thinking about whether you have credibility. But credibility plays a major role in how your message is received by your audience. Imagine if your audience hears your name and thinks, *She never wastes my time; her presentations are always to the point and relevant to what I need.* Now, imagine that your name gets this reaction: *his meetings usually run late, I'm never quite sure why we are taking this meeting, and I don't think he knows or cares about our business goals.* Who do you think is going to have a better chance of success?

As you consider your credibility, ask yourself:

1. How well does the audience know me?
2. What do they need to know about me?

3. Am I reliable?
4. How can I boost my credibility?
5. How will I connect with the audience?
6. How have I/we performed for them in the past?
7. What has their experience with me or my company or my predecessor been?

You can have a loss of credibility because of communication failures of your own, but you can also have a loss of credibility because you are taking over a project that has been beset with problems, or because you simply have never interacted with your audience before. Or maybe you know that you are delivering an unpopular message. Or your audience is in the room unwillingly. Or maybe you lack credibility because your company, or your industry, lacks credibility.

Without taking the time to analyze ahead of your presentation, you might never even think about these issues—and have no chance to rectify them. But by applying the Leverage Mindset, you can be more aware of any problems with your credibility and set out to address them.

For instance, if your audience doesn't know you well, consider contacting a mutual acquaintance who might be willing to recommend you. You could ask a colleague who does have good relationships in the audience to come with you to support the presentation. You might reach out for a "getting to know you" conversation before the meeting. If you know that someone in the room is already skeptical, consider meeting with them ahead of time to address their concerns. Of course, credibility grows when you actually deliver meaningful, productive communication. But there's much you can do ahead of time to add to the force at the end of your lever.

The Elephant in the Room

There are times when I go into a workshop knowing that the participants have been required to attend. That can be a big hurdle to having a great experience. I've learned to start with a question: 'How many of you are here against your will?' Sometimes people are honest and raise their hands, sometimes the question simply gets a laugh. But either way, I've addressed the elephant in the room—not everyone wants to be part of corporate training. At that point, I can say, "You don't have to be psyched to be here. But my job is to make sure that you have a good day." Once I acknowledge the dynamic, I have more credibility as a coach, and we can work together to make our time in the room productive. You can't beat honesty for credibility-building.

Why This Chapter is Important

If you've worked your way through these steps, congratulations. You are ready to move forward, and the rest of the process will be much easier because of the groundwork you've laid here.

Perhaps, though, you're skeptical. Maybe you are saying to yourself, "I don't have time to do all this—my presentation is tomorrow! I need to get to work on my slide deck!"

We're all tempted to cut corners when time is of the essence. But the work of this chapter actually makes the rest of your presentation *easier* and *faster* to pull together. And all the steps I lay out here can actually be completed in just a few minutes, especially once you've put them into practice a few times.

First, listen. While you want to approach listening with purpose as part of your presentation, I'm not actually creating a new step for you here; it's simply a way to make time you spend anyway more effective and productive for you.

Second, analyze. The beauty of the Leverage Mindset is that it is just that: a mindset. Once you've practiced asking yourself a few pointed questions to understand your own strengths and weaknesses heading into a communication opportunity, they will simply become a natural mindset. And knowing where you need more work or less work as you prepare your communication will ultimately save you time and effort.

From here, you'll begin to craft a clear, direct message; reinforce your key information with visual documents; and eliminate distraction and build confidence and authority in your delivery. With the mindset cultivated in this first skill area, you are well on your way to purposeful, powerful, persuasive communication.

Crafting a Persuasive Message

Many years ago, I was hired to coach a young rising executive, Matt, at a big insurance company. He'd been promoted from within to run a major portion of the business. His predecessor had retired and was a beloved figure in the office: the kind of leader who likes to walk the hallways, get to know everyone in the company, knows everyone's kids' names, and generally keeps morale high. But the division's performance had begun to slip a little bit, and company leadership felt a change within the business unit was necessary. Matt had been brought in because he had a background as an actuary and was laser focused on numbers and driving results.

I had known Matt's predecessor, but when I got the call to come in and coach, I didn't know anything about Matt. My HR contact told me that Matt's first couple of months had been rocky, and that his first all-hands meeting, in particular, had not gone well. The leadership of the company had begun to question whether he was the right person for the job.

Before I met with Matt, I asked him to send me the text of the speech from the all-hands meeting. On its face, the speech was pretty good, and its message focused on all the things Matt had been hired to do: get the business back to basics and boost their numbers.

When we met, I asked him to tell me about the meeting and how he felt about his speech. "I thought it was a good speech," he said. "But I got really negative feedback."

I asked him who was in the hall; he told me that the entire business unit was there, either in the room or on the phone—several hundred employees. I picked out a few key phrases from the speech: "more efficient," "streamlining," "shareholder value." "When your employees hear you leading with these phrases, what do you think they hear?" I asked. "If you put yourself in their shoes, you might see that when they hear those phrases, what they really hear is 'layoffs.' And once they hear 'layoffs,' that's the only thing they're going to hear throughout the rest of the speech."

"But those things are my mandate!" he protested. "That's what I was hired to do."

What Matt wasn't seeing was that his message needed to be aligned with his audience. The speech he wrote would have been great for a group of Wall Street investors. But for his employees, the people whose jobs were perceived to be at stake, the speech only stoked fear. Matt had only thought about what he wanted to say, not what he wanted to accomplish or how to align his goal with that of his audience. He'd thought about his own mandate—to get the division's numbers up. But he hadn't thought about his goal for this speech: to create a shared sense of purpose and a common mission to achieve better performance. To meet that objective, he needed to clarify his goal, understand his audience and their perspective, and plan his communication to bring these two elements together.

Message is everything. Without a concise, clear, audience-appropriate message, everything else is superfluous. Have a beautiful slide deck? Useless, if it's not supporting a strong message. Great speaking voice and charismatic presence? Sure, that might make you more superficially skillful, but without substance behind it you won't get far: great presence without a great message quickly will be exposed as empty.

What is message? It's not just knowing what you want to say. As Matt found out, you can put together a speech that sets out information precisely and emphatically, but still fails as persuasive communication. **Remember, we don't want to be messengers—we want to be persuaders, influencers, leaders.** A truly effective message is one that clarifies your goal, assesses that goal from the perspective of the audience, and finds a way to connect your goal to theirs in a way that inspires action.

In the last chapter, I talked about listening as a way to connect with your audience and analyzing your strengths and weaknesses to enhance your chances of success. This is the foundation we'll use to start crafting a message. If you skipped the last chapter, I strongly urge you to go back and review that material—it will make pulling together your message faster, more efficient, and much more effective. In this chapter, we take what you learned from Assess to build your Message through the GAP Method and Story Board Method; in the appendix you'll find a checklist to help guide you through the process step-by-step.

THE GAP METHOD

The GAP Method—know your Goals, understand your Audience, map your Plan—helps you gather and organize the information essential to crafting an effective message. It provides a concrete set of questions and steps to guide you through persuasive communication. In today's world, we all drown in information and struggle to meet all of the demands on our time; don't underestimate the power of a tool that helps you identify, structure, and prioritize. The GAP Method does exactly that. It helps you organize your mind, which will help you in several ways later on.

Maybe you feel like you don't have time to stop and think through a set of questions. Maybe you feel like you can barely keep up now. Maybe it feels like I'm asking too much of you to walk through these steps. Don't despair. The beauty of the GAP Method is that it can be effective even when you only have a few minutes. Of course, having a few hours to really dig into these questions may be better. But the GAP Method isn't just a task list; it is a framework, a focused way to think deliberately about your goals, your audience, and your key points. And the more you do it, the more efficient you become in using it, and the more automatic the framework becomes—it's like your computer's system monitoring, doing essential technical work quietly in the background.

GOALS + AUDIENCE + PLAN = GAP Method

Goals

The Latimer Group had contracted for a couple of years with a small IT group that handled our technology needs in-house. They'd done a great job for us, and were smart, pleasant people to work with. Toward the end of our initial contract with them, the owners asked our team to go to lunch.

It was a lovely meal and we had a nice conversation. But they never directed the conversation toward anything business-related. They didn't ask how we could continue to work together, they didn't ask for referrals, they didn't propose new ways to use technology to drive our business forward. Taking our (at the time) three-person team out to lunch was a big expenditure for a small business, and they'd really gotten nothing out of it.

As we walked back to our office, I told my colleagues, "That was a huge missed opportunity for them." The IT company wanted to cultivate our business relationship and knew that scheduling a meeting was a way to do that. But they didn't think through what they wanted to accomplish in that meeting, why we were all there, and how they needed to approach the conversation to achieve their goal.

Think about when you head out for a hike. Before you step foot on a trail, you decide on your destination, so that you know the direction you need to head. You identify some mile markers along the path so that you can gauge your progress and make sure you get to where you want to be, while giving yourself the flexibility to wander in between.

When you craft your message, you need to identify your ideal end result, and you need to figure out the key points that might get you there—your message mile markers. You don't need to always take the same path from point to point. But by making sure to hit each key point, you measure your progress toward your final destination—an effective, memorable message.

It's important to start by asking questions like: *what do I want to accomplish?* With your outcome in sight, you can more efficiently evaluate the information that will take your audience where you want them to go. This goal should be as specific as possible: what exactly do you want your audience to do once they leave your meeting? For every piece of information you gather, ask yourself, "Does this get me closer to my goal today?" If the answer is no, discard it. If yes, where does it lead you?

Bear in mind that, even for something as simple as a status report, you do have a goal. Maybe that goal is just to convince your boss to leave you alone, because you are doing a fine job. Don't fool yourself that an informational presentation doesn't need the same kind of thoughtful preparation as a sales pitch or a budget proposal.

Goals: Questions to Ask

- What are my goals?
- How do I define success?
- What do I want my audience to do?
- What do I want them *not* to do?
- What do I want my audience to remember?
- How do I want my audience to feel?
- How timely is my goal—does it need to happen right away, or is it over the long-term?
- How controversial is my topic?
- What is my ideal outcome?

Audience

I'd been tapped as one of three candidates to coach a young executive at an oil and gas company. The executive asked to meet with each of us before deciding whom to hire. When the head of HR called to ask if I would be interested, I told her I was glad to be in the running, asked for the name of the executive, and asked if she'd be willing to speak to me once more before the meeting, after I'd done some initial prep work. She agreed.

I set out to follow the GAP Method. I knew my goal: to be hired. But I didn't know my competition, and I didn't know what was most important to my audience. I decided to assume that my competition would be strong where I was weak, and to prepare accordingly. As for my audience, I first spent some time with the company website, looking at how they described themselves, what services they provided, what phrases recurred. I noticed repeated references to the technical nature of their work and the experience in the industry that it required—and that they believed they had.

Then I dug a little deeper. I looked at the bios of all the executives and noticed that they all talked about the deep experience of the leadership team. There it was again! Industry expertise was clearly important. Then I checked out the public trading information and noticed that they'd suffered a big hit a couple of years earlier, just after the BP disaster, when they'd had their own safety issues and the stock market had punished them for it. So clearly everyone in the company would be sensitive to issues of security and safety.

Finally, I looked at the young executive's LinkedIn page. I noticed that he'd gone to the same graduate program as a friend of mine. I called my friend and asked if he had any insight. He told me that one class they'd taken was about how to build a management team, and how important industry experience was in that effort. "Be ready for him to ask you about any other experience you've had in this field," he told me.

I called back the head of HR. Among other questions, I asked what mattered most to the executive when hiring. Once again, industry experience appeared at the top of the list.

So now I knew my biggest weakness: I had no industry experience at all. In order to be as competitive as possible, I had to assume that my competition did *have that experience. I also knew my strength: strong strategic skills and communication expertise and demonstrated success in coaching executive clients to be powerful, persuasive speakers. So the challenge became, how could I minimize what the executive might perceive as a weakness and display my strengths as a coach?*

I could say, "I don't have any experience but I'm a quick learner." But why would he pay me to learn on the job when he could just hire someone who already knew it?

Or, I could try to come up with some kind of transitive experience to obscure my lack of industry knowledge. But that would be easy to see through, and I didn't want to give the impression that I was trying to hide something.

Instead, I went to the meeting and said, directly, "You have an enormous amount of industry experience in your management team. You don't need any more industry experience. You have plenty. What you need from a coach is exactly what you cannot get from anyone else on your team. You need someone who can give you a fresh perspective." In positioning myself this way, I not only neutralized my lack of industry experience but also turned that perceived weakness into a significant strength. And by doing so, I also neutralized the advantage of industry experience that the other coaches might have.

Without the research that showed me what was important to my audience and what the executive likely would be thinking during our conversation, I couldn't have anticipated this potential objection. I wouldn't have addressed it head-on, and I couldn't have neutralized it. I would not have been hired.

Back to our hike. You know where you want to go. Now you need to invite a few people to come along, and you have the choice of a few different routes to the top. You have to know something about your companions in order to know how you'll get to your destination. Who has hiking experience? Who is recovering from a sprained ankle? Who likes to move quickly, or dawdle? All this is important information to make sure you can get to the end of the hike as a group.

In communication, we need to know our audience to know how to best carry them from key point to key point. The information we emphasize needs to be valuable to *them* in order to make sure their attention doesn't wander. You want everyone to stay with you, to the end.

Have you ever been in a meeting with someone who is clearly giving you the same presentation she's given before, to other audiences? There are some telltale signs: a generic set of benefits, little anticipation of objections, a lack of details that speak to your specific situation, and an inability to answer any question that strays too far from the prepared text. Chances are that you tuned out somewhere along the way because you didn't feel connected to what she was telling you. She wasn't talking to you, after all—she was just talking to a generalized someone.

When I say, "Know your audience," what do I really mean? For many people, just getting a list of who is going to be in the room suffices. Especially if they have communicated with the audience before—if the audience is a colleague or a client with whom the speaker has an existing relationship—no further thought seems necessary.

But the purpose of understanding your audience as part of the GAP Method is to drill down a bit more. If you are meeting an audience you don't know, a quick survey of LinkedIn will give you a starting point to understand a little more about them: educational background, current position, how long they've been at the company. If you do know the audience, it's arguably even more important to spend some time on this step. What might be new in their world? Do they have a new boss? Did they just get a promotion? Did their last project fail? All these things may have an impact on how they listen and react to your communication. Connecting with your audience is a key part of persuading your audience.

Spending time on understanding your audience during the GAP Method is an extension of the work you've already done in the Assess phase. Here, though, your work is more specific: how does your specific goal align with your specific audience, and in what ways might your audience receive or react to your message?

Think about the following:

Business context: Did their company just experience a significant rise or fall in their stock price? Has the leadership team been consistent, or have they had turnover recently? What is the organizational dynamic? Are they in a field that is intensely competitive?

Cultural context: Are there nuances of body language or tone of voice specific to their region or country? Is eye contact seen as connecting to the audience or challenging them? What kind of speaking style—assertive or deferential, direct or tactful—works best? Is there a particular corporate culture you should be aware of?

Personal context: Think about your audience: their background, experiences, or status within the company. Do they have particular needs that you can speak to? What anecdotes or supporting stories will be most effective? Will they be more receptive to a message that addresses a problem, or that presents an opportunity? Do you know of any special circumstances in their life: a military background, a new baby, a recent divorce? These might not come up in conversation, but knowing about them might make you more sensitive to your audience's state of mind.

Goals: As much as you have your goals in communication, your audience has their own goals. What are they trying to achieve as an organization or as an individual? Are their goals consistent or in conflict with yours?

Objections: Even as you search to find common ground, understanding points of disagreement may be even more important. If your audience fundamentally disagrees with you on one aspect of your proposal, you'll be unlikely to succeed if you haven't found a way to navigate that objection.

Decision-makers: Understanding who will ultimately say yes or no, and knowing whether he or she will be in the room, will change the way you frame your message. If the decision-maker is not in the room, you'll need to know who is going to report to that person—making sure the translator has the key information will be crucial.

By anticipating your audience's priorities, you can create a meaningful message, which will allow you to be more persuasive. You can better predict what will be valuable to the audience, or not; what their questions or objections will be; and the level of detail they will require.

Audience: Questions to Ask

- What are their goals? Can you tie your goal to theirs?
- What are their points of view?
  - Perceptions: What do they think of you, your organization, or your product?
  - Points of agreement: What is your common ground with the audience?
  - Value: Is there something that your audience wants that you can supply?
  - Objections: What will they hate? How firm are the objections?
- What will they like?
- What are their questions or objections?
- Are you speaking to the decision-maker or someone who reports to the decision-maker?

Plan

This final step is an output of the first two variables. You can't plan your hike without first determining where you want to go and who is going with you. But the plan—identifying all the mile markers along the way—is essential in ensuring that you make it to the end without losing any of your companions.

The outline you produce as part of this step will help clarify the key points you need to make along the way to your conclusion. These key points will then feed into a strong opening statement, a visually compelling slide deck, and the confidence and authority of your delivery—because you will know what you need to say and when in order to speak persuasively to your audience.

Make sure that you can articulate your key points clearly and succinctly. If you can't describe each one in a sentence (or less), keep refining. You'll plan out the message in more detail in the Story Board Method, but here you want to understand five key components to your message: the *what*, the *why*, the *how*, the *why not*, and the *next steps*.

The *What:* This may seem self-evident but distilling the reason for your communication is often an overlooked step. Know exactly and specifically what issue, opportunity, or problem you are addressing.

The *Why:* Remember, the *why* isn't about why *you* want to communicate to your audience; it is why *your audience* should want to listen to you. What's in it for them? Audiences won't listen just because you tell them to; they care about what you are saying. Make sure that you can explain it to them, quickly and directly.

The *How:* These are the details that support your message. This can be one of the trickiest elements for people to master—how to make sure you have enough detail to be convincing, but not so much that you lose the attention of your audience. An ability to determine what detail helps you to achieve your goal and what doesn't—the ability to spare your audience needless information, or the ability to synthesize a big data set into a simple summary—can be invaluable. For every piece of information, ask yourself, "Does this help me achieve my goal?" If the answer is yes, keep it in; if it is no, take it out; if you aren't sure, use other variables, such as your time constraints and your audience, to help you make a decision.

The *Why Not*: What will be the objections to your communication? Make sure you have a plan to address them, whether directly in your message plan, or more subtly (such as in a pre-meeting call). You may not be able to anticipate every objection but give some thought to the most likely culprits.

The *Next Steps:* You've done a great job with all the other components of your message plan. But without a clear directive of what needs to be done, who needs to do it, and when, the momentum of your persuasive message may be lost.

A participant at a workshop presented about a big new database project. He went through the benefits and the details of how it would work, but one detail never came up: how much it would cost. At the end, I asked the question, and he told us that it was a $30 million ask. For any business, that is a huge ask, and ignoring the size of the request won't make it go away.

After a few questions in this vein, it was clear that the presenter hadn't even thought about including the cost in his communication. He was focused on the benefits of his proposal: this was amazing technology that would make their business much more efficient and easier to use.

What he needed to remember is that, to his audience, cost was just as important as the benefits of the technology. He needed to anticipate the possible objection and structure his business case around the return on investment. For example: "This project requires a significant investment. This will cost $30 million in initial purchase, training, and start-up costs. However, in the first year alone we will save X amount of money in overhead and redundancy cost. Further, we'll avoid Y amount of risk and potentially generate Z dollars of new business."

Whenever we communicate, we have to make choices about what details to include and which to exclude. Take a few minutes to think about your audience and your goal. What are the details that will bring them into alignment? This assessment can make the difference between a Yes or a No.

Plan: Questions to Ask

- What is my persuasive point of view?
- Message outline:
  - WHAT do I want to say?
  - WHY should my audience listen?
  - HOW can I convince them?
  - WHY NOT follow my plan?
  - NEXT STEPS, who needs to do what, and when?

The stakes were high. A major multiyear contract, worth billions, was in play. The team pitching the company's bid knew they had to build a powerful case, but as they gathered their data, pulled together their plan of action, and asserted their years of experience, they never reached consensus on the central message of their presentation. Meanwhile, they'd already missed one deadline, so they felt they just didn't have time to slow down and assess the situation. They decided to focus on demonstrating their vast knowledge by putting up every metric and specification they could around the work they'd be doing.

When the day for the presentation arrived, the presenting team had assembled a two-hundred-slide deck and spoke to their audience for almost two hours. Each person was responsible for one element of the presentation, and their transitions were often abrupt and made little sense. While everyone focused on the ultimate goal of winning the contract, they didn't have a sense of the larger narrative of why each element they described added to their value proposition for the audience. At the end, the audience seemed overwhelmed and bored. They asked a few questions, but the pitch had clearly failed. Hundreds of hours of time were wasted, and a huge business opportunity was lost.

When the team reconvened after their failed pitch, the mood was bleak. Where had they gone wrong? First, they hadn't really understood what their audience was looking for. They weren't sure who was going to be in the room, and no one was really clear on what they needed or wanted— whether cost, expertise, or initiative was the driving factor in the decision-making. So all the information they had thrown up on the screen was just numbers and specs, lacking any context or driving purpose.

Second, they had failed to align all their separate messages toward a larger narrative that would help them to reach their goal: the major contract. The pieces weren't working together toward a greater purpose, and the effect on their audience was clear.

What they needed was a structure: to focus on the most important information, across all the individual presentations; to sequence each presentation in a way that built up a logical, persuasive case overall; and to close with a synthesis of what had come before and which reiterated the key points they wanted to get across.

THE STORY BOARD METHOD

Most people approach the sequencing of their communication linearly. They present their information from beginning to end, which culminates in the most important information finally appearing in the big conclusion.

This tendency is why it is so common to go to a meeting and see everyone flipping to the end of a slide deck when the presenter has just started speaking. The audience is thinking, "What's the point here, and what do I really need to know?"

Structuring a business communication is not about building suspense. We aren't looking for the next movie blockbuster. Attention spans are limited. Audiences just want to know the point and purpose of the meeting or the phone call.

We live in an on-demand world, where any piece of information is at our fingertips, and a multitasking world, in which we are more often than not juggling multiple screens, multiple tasks, and multiple priorities at any given time. In order to survive and thrive in this kind of environment, we have to be able to capture and keep attention.

The Story Board Method is a tool to do just that. In it, you'll structure and sequence a message in a way that engages your audience, delivers the appropriate level of detail, and closes powerfully and memorably. As with each step of the Latimer Model, we're seeking here to create connection. How can you get people to care about what you are saying and inspire them to action?

This structure builds on a classic three-act structure—a storytelling model that dates back to Aristotle and forms the basis of many novels, plays, and films. Here, though, we are using the structure to persuade rather than entertain.

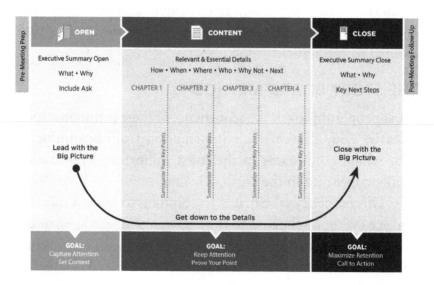

ACT ONE: Pull your audience in with a strong open. This is your first chance to engage with your audience and convince them that you are worth paying attention to. Give your audience a sense of what's to come, why they should care about what you are about to say, and what you are going to ask them to do.

Many of us rely on the agenda open as a reliable, easy way to set out what's to come. But an executive summary open can be more effective in not only setting out the topic clearly, but in stating your persuasive point of view, setting forward your recommendation (or ask), and quickly highlighting the key points to come.

ACT TWO: Make your case. Support your argument with the specific information—data, anecdotes, detailed studies—that can persuade your audience that you have the right plan. Giving this act a structure—a logical sequence of chapters, with internal summary along the way to remind your audience what's at stake—will make it easier for an audience to follow your argument and to remember the key information.

Throughout, bring life to your details by using anecdotes, strong statistics, and quantification of your argument. While you want to be aware of overwhelming your audience with too much information, you need to have enough to be convincing, persuasive, and memorable.

ACT THREE: Quickly and emphatically make your closing statement. In other words: repeat, repeat, repeat. Most audience members will have drifted off at some point in your presentation—this is your chance to reiterate your most important points in a succinct, memorable way. Make sure everyone in the room walks out knowing exactly what you are recommending and/or what you want them to do. If Act One and Act Three sound a lot alike—great. It may feel overly repetitive, but repetition is memorable—and highly effective.

The first day of our workshop, Maria stepped up to give her presentation on Employee Resource Groups. She jumped in with the details of what these groups entailed, then abruptly moved on to benefits that the company offered around work-life balance and stress management. The connection between these opportunities and the Employee Resource Groups didn't make much sense, as the latter had more to do with career development and networking. And her audience struggled to pay attention to content that didn't answer the fundamental question, "What's in it for me?"

Maria had made the mistake of treating her presentation like a lecture and forgot about making a connection with the audience. She focused on telling the audience what existed, rather than why it mattered. And she had lost sight of creating a logical structure and flow that would highlight key points clearly. Her delivery reflected the disorder. She seemed nervous and hesitant from the beginning and had to spend long moments looking back at her slides to remember what she wanted to say.

I suggested that she take a second look at her presentation through the prism of the Story Board Method. "Think about how to use your open to draw us in. Key points can become chapters. Then, take us out with a close that reiterates these main points and inspires us to action."

The next day, Maria gave the presentation again. This time, she used a vivid anecdote of networking to draw us in to her proposal. Then she clearly stated her goal: to get each one of us to consider joining an Employee Resource Group. She used her key points to structure the body of her presentation: the individual benefits, the organizational benefits, and the professional opportunities available. And she closed with a strong statement that urged us to get involved.

The difference in the two presentations was dramatic. Her audience understood immediately why this mattered to them. Maria connected her proposal to concrete benefits, both personal and organizational, and made the way to access those benefits immediately clear. Best of all, the clear structure allowed Maria to express herself more passionately, and her audience felt her commitment to and enthusiasm for this initiative.

Keeping It Short and Simple

How do you make sure that what you say is absolutely clear and that you don't lose your audience with long-winded descriptions or an overabundance of detail? In today's business world, we all have endless data at our fingertips. We can all drown in information if we want to. Gathering data is no longer so valuable—but summarizing it clearly and quickly is invaluable.

The most important strategy to be both clear and brief is to prepare. If we don't know what we want to say, and when we want to say it, our ability to convey information is highly compromised.

How can you prepare?

1. Ask yourself simple questions: "What is my goal?" "What am I recommending?" "Why should my audience agree to my solution?" "What do I need from my audience?"
2. Answer the questions simply. Be direct and concise. Make sure that you use these simple sentences in your presentation.
3. Remind yourself of the big picture. At every juncture of your presentation think about what you really want to accomplish. Don't get lost in the weeds. Have enough detail to support your argument but save the nitty-gritty for a handout or backup slides. Be prepared to get into relevant details for your audience during a Q&A.
4. Make your ending the beginning. Don't leave us in suspense—this isn't a novel or a movie. Your audience wants to know the point of the meeting. Don't make them flip to the end—put it in your very first slide.

The Accordion Presentation

You've been tasked with creating a presentation to convince an executive audience to invest in a new initiative. You'll have an hour, and you've carefully assessed your challenge, identified your goal, and mapped a persuasive presentation with all the metrics that support your recommendation. You are well prepared. But then, the day before the meeting, you step onto an elevator with the COO. "I'm glad I ran into you," she says. "I can't make it tomorrow—can you just give me a quick summary right now?"

No one loves being put on the spot this way. But if you've done your work well, you should be able to turn an hour-long presentation into a five-minute pitch without too much trouble.

The key is to think of your presentation as an accordion: your open and close—the summary of the problem, solution, and ask you are making of your audience—are the handles, and the details in the middle are the bellows, expanding and contracting based on the situation.

Of course, this isn't an easy or inborn skill. The following happens all the time in our workshops: a ten-minute presentation doesn't make a persuasive case, and the presenter protests, "Well, this was originally an hour-long presentation—I just couldn't fit it all into ten minutes!" The problem here is a tendency to get fixated on the details: the nitty-gritty of the costs, the process, or the implementation schedule. If you only have five or ten minutes, lots of those details need to fall away, and that can cause anxiety if you aren't prepared.

How can you prepare? Figuring out your accordion can be a good first step in constructing your longer presentation, because it forces you to distill your argument into simple, direct language. Start by asking yourself some questions, and restrict yourself to a single sentence in answering them:

1. What's the problem/situation?
2. What's my solution/opportunity?

3. What do I need from my audience?
4. Why is it in their best interest to at least listen?

These four questions can form your open. If you have more time, you might add a compelling anecdote or attention-grabbing statistic. For an elevator pitch, these four sentences will likely suffice.

Now, what are the key points that support your assessment of the problem and the solution? How do you get from one to the other? As you make these key points, you can add supporting detail/statistics as you have time.

Finally, reiterate your summary. Even in a short presentation, repetition helps your audience to take away exactly what you need.

Once you have this simplified structure, you can build around it, focusing on the details that support your argument or explain your solution. These details are important and valuable, and you always want to be able to draw on the specifics and statistics that support your recommendation. But having a clear idea of your summary and your key points gives you a strong structure, a sharp vision of what you need your audience to take away, and the flexibility to persuade someone in the boardroom or while walking down the hall. Your accordion can be stretched or compressed to any size, and your persuasive power will be the same no matter how much time you have.

Business Storytelling

Ashley had prepared a presentation for a workshop about her company's inventory analysis software. She was an IT manager, and took a technical approach to her ask, presenting four options for handling the software that were filled with specs, acronyms, and performance metrics that almost no one else in the room knew how to decipher.

Ashley took the feedback from that workshop and redid her presentation. This time, she structured it around an analogy. "Think of this system as our house. Our house needs some work. The floors are warped; the windows won't shut all the way; our fixtures and appliances are all outdated. So we have four options. One: We can tear down the house and rebuild—in other words, we can build a new system to replace this one. Two: We can renovate the house bit by bit— we can keep handling our current system with patchwork fixes. Three: We can just move out and find a new place—we can buy a new system that someone else has built. Four: We can do nothing and live with the problems."

By taking out the technical content and using an analogy that anyone could relate to, Ashley connected with her audience and created a perspective for her proposal that was both compelling and persuasive.

Business storytelling can be a highly effective technique. Humans are story-driven creatures, and even highly technical content can be conveyed persuasively through narrative. Of course, this carries a risk too—we don't want to seem to be treating sensitive or cost-intensive topics flippantly. The key is to treat storytelling with the same purposefulness as you would treat a more conventional presentation.

First, consider your **goal**. What do you want to accomplish with your story?

Second, identify the **key takeaways** that you want to reinforce.

Third, decide what **kind of story** will work best: personal, professional, success, lesson learned?

Fourth, think about what kind of **emotion** you want to elicit from your audience.

You can map out your story by breaking it down into four main elements:

Protagonist: Who is the main character?

Catalyst: What compels the protagonist to take action?

Turning Point: What is the discovery, epiphany, or crucial event that changes the course of events?

Resolution: What does the protagonist learn from these events?

Throughout this process, keep in mind the relevance of your story and each detail to the topic and the goal of your communication. While the purpose of storytelling is to engage and connect, it needs to be in service of inspiring action in your audience.

CASE STUDY: Antonio

Using GAP and the Storyboard Method to make a dense presentation meaningful and engaging

Antonio was preparing for a major presentation to his CEO that outlined the near and long-term goals for his unit. Antonio's unit was a new addition to the structure of this multibillion-dollar company, and justifying their strategic function was crucial in order for them to stay in operation and receive the necessary budget to fulfill their objectives.

Antonio wanted to cover a lot of ground in the presentation, starting with the establishment of his unit, reminding his audience of the work they'd done and what they'd accomplished, setting out the goals over the next year, and establishing a vision for the five years beyond that. He set to work gathering his materials for each of these sections.

He knew a lot was on the line, so once he'd pulled everything together, he asked a small team of colleagues to listen to his presentation and give him some feedback. They convened in a small conference room. Antonio felt relaxed in front of these peers, and he knew his material cold, so he spoke with confidence and conviction.

Even so, he sensed an immediate disengagement in his audience. These were colleagues who were intimately familiar with the context of the unit's work, and painfully aware of the importance of this presentation. Yet no one seemed fully attuned to what he was saying, and the energy of the room was low. What was happening?

Antonio made it to the end of his presentation and concluded with a call for questions and a quick thank you for their time. He took a deep breath and asked for some feedback.

"I thought you had some interesting history, but I wasn't sure where you were going with it. I have to admit, I lost track of what you were talking about pretty quickly."

"I didn't understand why we were in the room. And it was hard for me to keep track of where we were in the presentation."

"I felt like the presentation just stopped. I didn't even realize you were done until you said, 'Thank you for your time.'"

What happened?

Antonio had been meticulous in gathering his details. He knew the goal of his presentation. But he hadn't thought about how to structure his information so that the details fully supported his goal and connected his audience meaningfully to what needed to be done.

When he looked again at what he'd put together, he realized that he'd simply started from the beginning—when the unit had been pulled together and why—and progressed chronologically from there, culminating in the one- and five-year plans. He hadn't thought about how to open in a way that would grab his audience's attention and set the context for why they should want to listen to him.

Antonio needed to start by asking himself a few questions:

- What is the overarching message of his presentation?
- What overall goal does he want to achieve?
- What are the key points he needs to hit?
- What details enrich and support those key points?
- What action items does he need to convey to his audience?

Since his presentation ran for almost forty-five minutes, Antonio also needed to think about using internal summaries—reiteration of his overarching message at the end of each chapter, so that every step of the presentation felt like a part of a whole. Once he clarified his goal, he needed to make sure that his audience understood how each piece of the presentation supported and was essential to that goal.

The Presentation

After spending some time really understanding the message he wanted to articulate and how to best sequence his information, Antonio felt prepared.

When he came into the room, he began by summarizing the purpose of the unit, the short-term goals for their performance, and their long-term vision for how to add productivity and centralized strategic support across multiple business units.

As he moved through specific sections devoted to the unit's history, past successes, current initiatives, and future projects, he continually referred back to how each of these demonstrated the unit's commitment to strategic support. Every data point and statistic tied back to that overarching goal.

In conclusion, he restated the objective purpose of his presentation, the unit's strong performance and ambitious plans for strategic support, and reasserted what he needed from his audience to continue this important work.

As he spoke, he noticed that the CEO nodded along at key moments, and even scribbled down a few notes. Afterward, the CEO pulled Antonio aside to ask a few follow-up questions. A few days later, Antonio heard from his boss; the unit had been given the budget they needed to implement their next steps.

Antonio made a few crucial moves. First, his preparation included a dry run, which allowed him to identify major flaws *before* it really counted. Second, he spent time to clarify his goal and identify the best way to communicate that goal to his audience. Finally, he made sure to clearly and repeatedly tie his content back to that goal, so that his message was unified and strengthened throughout. Each of these steps increased his odds of success and helped him convey complex information in a way that was easy to understand and persuasive.

CHAPTER 5

Making it Visual

When we walk into a room to communicate with an audience, we have at our fingertips a powerful tool—powerful, but also risky and often misused. That tool is PowerPoint.

When we do it well, we offer reinforcement of our spoken message, a visual shortcut to recognizing its key points, and a valuable way to boost retention. But when we do it wrong, we risk cognitive overload: asking our audience to read too much text, figure out a confusing graphic, or ignore a mishmash of fonts and styles. If your audience is doing any of those things, they're likely distracted and not listening to you.

I've learned from years of teaching workshops that nearly everyone starts their preparation for a presentation by planning a slide deck, whether that means opening up a new PowerPoint, repurposing an old one or two (which often results in a Frankenstein-like creation of mismatched fonts, colors, header placement, and even slide numbers), or adapting a colleague's work. (Some organizations have revolted and turned against slide decks, as I note later in the chapter, but PowerPoint still dominates most corporate settings.) After all, getting your slide deck together first gives you a pleasing sense of structure, a feeling that you've organized your thoughts, and a reassuring sense that, if nothing else, you've got *something* to show at this presentation.

To that I say: Stop!

Your slide deck MUST be a continuation and reflection of the analysis you did in your first skill area, Assess (chapter 3) and the message construction from the second skill area, Message (chapter 4). If you skipped those chapters in favor of this one—go back. If you don't understand the challenge ahead of you, if you don't have any insight into your audience, if you haven't clarified your goal, if you haven't identified your key points, you will not be able to reflect those in your slides. And remember: as with every element of persuasive communication, you *must* think about documenting from the perspective of the audience. What is going to help build their retention, spark recognition, and get the response and inspire the action you want?

For our purposes, the Document step generally focuses on a slide deck because, for better or worse, PowerPoint is the most common method of documentation in modern business culture. However, a document could also mean a handout, an email, or any other visual representation of your message.

As you begin the process of documenting, three things are important to keep in mind:

1. Context is key. I like to offer guidelines for what makes for a strong slide deck. But only *you* know what your audience needs. Some audiences want more data points in their slides, some audiences want simple, powerful images. I don't speak in absolutes because every audience is different—but make sure that you spend some time considering what will work best in your situation.

2. Slides are for your audience, not for you. If you find yourself saying, "I don't want to forget to discuss this point, so I'll include it on the slide," put down the PowerPoint and walk away. *Slides are not a script.* Nothing should show up on the slide that isn't there to help your audience understand your message.

3. Minimize distractions. Remember that you've just put a lot of care, thought, and work into your message. If you create cognitive overload for your audience—through

too much text, overly complex graphics, vague or imprecise slide headers or key-point boxes, or visual inconsistencies—you'll undermine all that work.

Documents can be powerful supporting players in conveying your message persuasively. When you walk into a room, you may not know what kind of learning styles might be present. Some people may zone out when they have to listen for an extended period of time; others may not find the visual presentation of information memorable. By marrying visual imagery or a written reiteration of your key points to a verbal presentation, you have a better chance at capturing a bigger portion of your audience. And if they *do* tune out, strong, easy-to-follow slides give them an on-ramp back into the presentation. But you must approach this document thoughtfully in order for it to be a benefit rather than a risk. (In the appendix, you'll find a checklist of questions—"Document Effectiveness Review"— that can help guide you through this process.)

No Slides Without Message

There is no piece of advice I have that is more important than this:

You cannot create a powerful, meaningful slide deck without a strong, clear message.

If you skipped chapter 4, go back! (And when you get there, you'll see that I advise you not to skip chapter 3, either.) Spending even a few minutes thinking through your message will save you a great deal of time and energy in putting together a slide deck that will resonate with your audience and help boost the retention of your key points.

Bonus: if you go through the entire Story Board process outlined in chapter 4, you can almost auto populate the headers of your slide deck with the key points you identify as part of your Act 2.

Help Your Audience Recognize and Retain

Perhaps the most important function of your document is to help your audience to *recognize* and *retain* your key messages. I've mentioned the information-saturated, multitasking, short-attention-span world we live in, and the fight we all wage to make an impact with our communication. The beauty of a slide deck or other document is that it can take advantage of the human brain's rapid visual processing to spark recognition and capture attention. And when something has captured our attention, we are more likely to remember it later.

No audience remembers 100 percent of what they hear. Most people believe a listener's retention rate lands somewhere between 10 and 25 percent. Whatever the true percentage, we know that not everything we say will be recalled. But slides, in reiterating our message visually, can boost our chances of having our audience remember the most important information.

Our brains are powerful visual processors, able to consume visual information in milliseconds. Attaching an image to a word or name is a well-known memorization trick. But not just any image will work. You need to make sure that it is logical, simple, and immediately—yes—recognizable.

Of course, you need to always make sure that your slide deck is not overshadowing you, the speaker. When your audience looks at a slide, it is important that they are able to recognize and understand its meaning within a few seconds. Any more than that and they are no longer listening to you—they are trying to puzzle out what exactly they are looking at.

For this reason, be as concise as possible. Reading is an automatic distraction. Images are typically more accessible and more memorable but apply your audience awareness. You need to know what will resonate with your audience, either because of a familiar association or because it aligns well with your message. Goofy clip art, complicated imagery, or esoteric allusions will all work against you.

When you think about a great slide for recognition, think about slides that can be understood at first glance. A short, concise bullet-point list; a powerful, simple image; a takeaway box. When your audience can take in the valuable information from the slide almost instantly, they can immediately return to listening to the information you are telling them verbally.

If you have a slide that is more dense—whether it is a slide that you've been mandated to use, or you have an audience that wants and appreciates a high level of detail—you can still think about ways to make the key point easily accessible and recognizable. Key-point boxes, strategic use of color or highlighting, or animations can all bring the most important information into focus.

Slides can help create a visual reference for people to draw on when they want to remember what you discussed. If you have good audience awareness, you can connect an image to their prior knowledge, which will make it even more memorable. Consider what will be meaningful to your audience, and what they might already know about the information you are presenting. Then, speak to its importance directly and clearly.

When you've created a powerful message that aligns with powerful visuals, you'll see a great boost in the retention of your key points.

Death by PowerPoint—or Death to PowerPoint?

As much as we rely on PowerPoint, most of us also bemoan it. At times we feel overwhelmed by an avalanche of clip art, animations, bullet points, and densely detailed charts and graphs. Some estimate that more than thirty million

PowerPoint presentations are given *each day*. No wonder "Death by PowerPoint" has become a cultural touchstone.

The stultifying slide deck is usually a product of focusing on your documentation rather than on your message. Or maybe you rely on your slides to keep your place through the presentation, so that your slides function more as your own script than as a tool for your audience. Or maybe you have six slides for every minute of your presentation, so that you are clicking through faster than anyone could ever absorb the information. (This often originates in confusion between a slide deck and a handout; for more on this see "What Kind of Document Do You Need?" in this chapter.)

The PowerPoint deck has earned such a bad reputation that some companies are moving to ban it altogether. At Amazon, executive presenters provide a multipage narrative memo before a meeting; LinkedIn executives are encouraged to forgo the slide deck as well. Leaders in the military, physicists, and intelligence chiefs have all spoken out about the deadening effects of presenting information through slides. General James Mattis put it bluntly: "PowerPoint makes us stupid."

But is it PowerPoint's fault, or our own? After all, even Jeff Bezos admits that moving to memos doesn't solve the problem of poor communication—a six-page narrative can also be badly organized, too wordy, and poorly thought through. Whether we are writing a memo or putting together a slide deck, we first have to assess the communication opportunity before us and construct a clear, concise message.

Once we've done that, PowerPoint *can* be a powerful tool. (And make no mistake—PowerPoint remains the mode of documentation for most organizations.) Humans respond viscerally to images, and we process visual information sixty-five thousand times faster than text. A vivid image that connects to our message can be much more memorable than a paragraph of text.

We don't *have* to sacrifice PowerPoint to save ourselves.

Know Your Tech

Nothing can cause a presentation to go awry like unexpected or malfunctioning technology. A new kind of clicker, an LED screen that doesn't reflect a laser pointer, a projector that washes out your colors, a laptop loaded with a different version of the software—all these things can undermine the deck you've put so much thought into and throw off your entire presentation.

There's a lot of new technology in presentation spaces that can be amazing to take advantage of, but you have to know what's going to be available to you. It's another facet of your research—what's the space going to be like? Will you have a touch screen? Will you be able to look at your laptop screen as the slides are projected behind you? What will be the screen aspect ratio? Will you have wireless internet access? Will the laptop be connected to a new, high-def screen, or an old-school projector?

Asking these questions before you start building your deck will save you time and avoid undermining your credibility.

What Kind of Document Do You Need?

How many times have you attended a meeting where the slide deck is exactly the same as the handout that you receive (or that is emailed out later)? Maybe your company insists on using the slide deck as a handout, or it just seems easier to have one document do double duty.

Slides and handouts, though, should be considered separate, if related, documents. After all, the goals are not the same. In slides, the visual representation of your message is supporting your delivery without distracting from it; a good slide often can't stand on its own but requires you to speak to its relevance. In handouts, details are important, and you need to be able to write out connections clearly and directly so that anyone can understand your message without having heard you speak.

What's more, there are different degrees of detail between a primarily visual slide deck and a text-heavy handout. I break these down into four general categories of document; it's up to you to assess your audience's needs and decide which is best for your particular presentation.

Presentation slide deck: This type of document supplements you as a speaker and contains only high-level detail. The content emphasizes visual recognition: images, simple graphs, single-line bullet points.

Leave-behind slide deck: This document still primarily supplements your speaking, and enhances your message, but includes enough detail so that someone who missed the meeting can follow along. However, large, finely detailed data sets or large chunks of text should not be included.

Handout: This type of document encompasses the entirety of your message, in as much detail as necessary. Handouts can allow you to provide extensive background, large sets of data and analysis, and more in-depth detail, which an audience can absorb on their own time.

Combination: This includes both a primarily visual presentation deck and a more detailed handout. This is best used when a key decision maker can't be present, or if you know that your message will need to be shared more widely in the organization.

Bear in mind that, when you are speaking to an audience, what matters most is that they have the capacity to *listen*; if they are busy reading, they can't physiologically attend to what you are saying. That's just how our brains work. A powerful slide deck reinforces the message coming out of your mouth, in the way that speaks most directly to your audience's needs, without competing with you for the audience's attention.

Frame, Fill, Finish

You've decided which kind of document best supports your message and meets the expectations of your audience. Now, how do you go about creating a slide deck that facilitates recognition and retention?

The Latimer Group's Document Construction Model sets out a three-part process to create documents: Frame, Fill, Finish. Helpfully, you've already done much of the work—the Story Board Method (described in chapter 4) has created the outline that should translate easily into a document framework, while the details you've chosen to support your persuasive message can be used to flesh out that skeleton. Finally, you need to spend some time looking carefully and critically at the overall presentation of the document, so that you can eliminate any potential distractions.

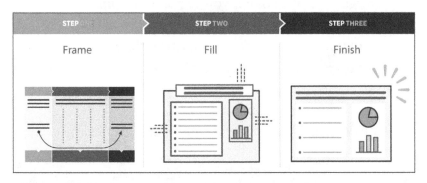

Frame

I met a team in financial services who wanted help refining their slide deck in their initial presentations to potential new clients. They felt like they made a strong case for their expertise and their track record, but they were failing to close as many clients as they wanted. I asked to see the current slide deck, and they pulled out a PowerPoint that ran to seventy-five slides. Each slide was dense with information: detailed allocation breakdowns, historical performance data, projected outcomes over time.

All this was important information for a client seeking to hire financial services. But it was also information that they might better absorb on their own time, without someone also speaking to them. We worked over a few days to hone their high-level story, and we lifted out the nitty-gritty to put into a separate handout. We focused on finding visual representations of their narrative and distilling the key points into single bullet-point takeaways. By the end of our work, we'd cut the deck to ten powerful slides—and the team saw their rate of closing soar.

The structure of a slide deck—the overall message, key points, and logical flow—is a crucial but often overlooked element. It's not enough to identify what material can be represented visually, or to pull in slides from an old deck that cover the same ground.

The good news is that if you've put in the time to structure your message, you've already got the skeleton of the slide deck in front of you. With the Story Board Method (see chapter 4), you've figured out the three acts of your message, the key points and essential details, and the final action items. Your slide deck echoes and supports this outline.

For example, you might frame your slide deck this way:

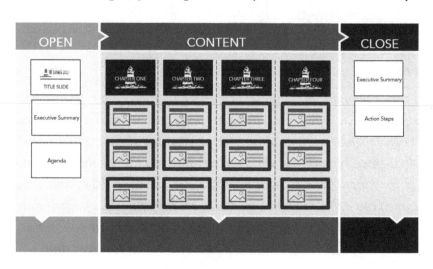

By giving thought to your structure, you'll be thinking about how you lead your audience through your ideas, which will help you have smoother, more polished transitions.

One question I often field: how many slides should I have in my deck? There's no magic number—remember, context is everything here—but a general metric holds that your number of slides should roughly equal half the presentation time. So if, for instance, you are presenting thirty minutes of content, preparing fifteen slides would be a good starting point.

With this starting point in mind, the following variables can help you determine if more or fewer slides might be necessary for your specific audience and presentation.

MORE SLIDES	FEWER SLIDES
The topic is new and unfamiliar.	The topic is well-known and familiar.
The topic is controversial.	The topic is relatively benign.
The topic presents bad news.	The topic presents good news.
Your audience is skeptical.	Your audience has already shown support.

Keep in mind one absolute: as you approach a one-to-one ratio (i.e., thirty slides for a thirty-minute presentation), you become more likely to overwhelm your audience with too much information.

As you wrap up the Frame portion of document construction, make sure that you've thought about the following elements:

- How many slides should I have?
- How should I sequence the story?
- How many slides should be in each section?
- Is this structure logical and persuasive?

Then it's time to move on to filling out the content.

When the Slides are Out of Your Control

I often run into the following scenario, especially in fields that are heavily regulated and that need strict compliance oversight. A workshop participant gives a presentation that fails to set context, gets mired in detail, and closes without a clear sense of purpose or next steps. When I begin to get into this feedback, the person's defense is often, "But this is the slide deck I have to use."

My response is simple: you may not be able to control the slide deck, but you can control the narrative.

Be flexible: If you can't add an executive summary slide, take some time, with the title slide up, to share a summary of your narrative.

Change what you can: Sometimes you can move dense slides to backup or switch up the order to better fit your narrative. Find out where you can take some liberty and where you can't and use that to your advantage.

Acknowledge a busy slide: Compliance requires you to have the slide that shows your twenty-year performance record—a full slide of tiny numbers. Don't be afraid to say, "I know this is an overwhelming slide, but I want you to just focus on these key numbers."

As one of my clients once noted in a workshop, "A slide template is not a message plan." Whether you have a strict template you have to work within or a prescribed deck, your slide deck shouldn't dictate your message. Craft a powerful, persuasive message first, and the constraints of your slide deck will matter less.

Fill

Closely aligned with the structure of your slide deck is the message of each slide and the deck as a whole. While structure relates to the logical flow from idea to idea, the message has to do with slide content—the words, images, and ideas you want to use to support what you are saying.

Many people fall into the trap of "more is more"; they try to capture every detail of their presentation in a slide. But no one is able to both read a complex slide and listen to what the presenter is trying to say about it. Sometimes people do this because they are using their slides as a script—but no one wants to sit in a room while someone reads off the screen to them. It's a waste of time—most people can read a slide faster than you can read it to them—and diminishes your value as a speaker because you aren't adding anything to what people can already see on the screen. Further, it severs your connection to the audience, because I can guarantee you aren't making any eye contact.

The content of your slides should support your mission to help your audience to Recognize and Retain your message and key points. People need to know why to pay attention, why it is important, and why it is relevant to them.

Use titles and headers strategically: It's easy to fall into the trap of using generic titles or headers that are accurate, but don't tell your audience much about your message. Yet these titles and headers are valuable real estate, and your audience will likely notice them before anything else on the slide. Think about giving these elements a point of view that supports your goal. For instance, rather than using the slide header "Analysis," try something like, "Improving Efficiency." Instead of calling your presentation "Quarterly Review," signal the discussion to come by calling it "Solving Customer Retention Problem." Simple, direct titles and headers can help you cut through the noise.

Use a mix of visual elements and text: Your audience will include a group of people that may all receive information differently. Some may be visual, others may absorb information by listening, and others may need both. So, whenever possible, use a combination of images and text. This combination will provide further understanding and context for your audience.

Be concise: Avoid complete sentences and keep bullet points to a single line. What's up on the screen is a visual aid to the audience, not a way to remember your secondary and tertiary points.

It's useful to think of slides as signposts on a trail. You have to get to each signpost—your key points—but how you get there isn't as important. Don't map out every footstep.

Eliminate unnecessary slides: For each slide, try to finish these two statements: "I'm including this slide because…" and "The key point on this slide is…" If you can't immediately end those sentences, get rid of the slide or, at a minimum, put it in the back-up section.

Repeat, and then repeat again: As with your message, crafting a strong, simple opening and closing slide can help ensure that your key points come through loud and clear. Everyone is busy, and everyone is overloaded with meetings. The more easily your audience can walk away with a two- or three-sentence summary of your presentation in their head, the more persuasive you will be.

Prepare for questions: If you put a statistic, a graph, a chart, or a reference on a slide, be prepared to field questions on it. If you aren't prepared to give more context or defend what you have on the slide, consider taking it off (or spend more time preparing).

As I've said before, persuasive, outcome-oriented communication is all about connection. Your slide deck shouldn't act as a wall between you and your audience. It should offer another avenue to demonstrate your awareness of their concerns and context and forge a bridge between what *you* want from your audience and what *they* need.

I got a call from an HR contact in a client company—a new, high-potential executive, Ahmed, needed coaching. While he was clearly smart and talented, he kept losing control of the meetings he ran, and it was starting to make people question his leadership. He needed help with meeting facilitation.

Before I began coaching, I asked if I could come in and observe Ahmed run a meeting. When I arrived, I sat in the back of a large room—around thirty people were there. Ahmed was a good speaker, and he clearly articulated his message and his key points. But when it was time for the Q&A, he lost control of the room.

When I met with Ahmed afterward, I told him, "You're a great speaker. But you don't need better facilitation skills."

He looked surprised.

"You need help with your slide deck," I told him. Ahmed had a lot of extraneous detail on his slides, I explained, and that made it easy for his audience to derail the discussion with questions that were irrelevant to what he wanted to talk about. "You're giving them mental off-ramps, and that's what is making the meeting feel out of control."

Ahmed and I worked on tightening up the content of his slides; instead of including a full set of data, including numbers that had nothing to do with his message, we focused only on the statistics that were directly relevant to what he wanted to say that day. With a slide deck as tightly controlled as his message, Q&A became a productive discussion, rather than a digressive battle, and no one had difficulty seeing Ahmed as a leader in his company.

Finish

Looks aren't everything—but when it comes to slides, you need to spend adequate time making sure that your slides are clean, consistent, and legible. Remember, slides offer much risk, because there will invariably be someone in the room who delights in pointing out a spelling mistake or a misplaced header. (I once heard the story of a client who received only one piece of feedback for his presentation: "You used the wrong shade of blue.") At the same time, when done well, slides can powerfully reinforce your message.

Consistency is key: The cleaner and more precise your slides are, the more impact their information will have—the focus stays on the substance, not on a logo that floats from spot to spot. The reverse is also true: an audience tends to see a sloppy deck as a reflection of a sloppy mind. If the slides look thrown together, how rigorous can the analysis be?

It's not uncommon to use slides from multiple decks to create a new presentation. As long as the message on those slides matches the message you have crafted for this particular communication, fine. But make sure that you align your formatting, keep your font consistent, and renumber your slides. (There's no bigger tell than when you jump from slide 3 to slide 42 to slide 15.)

Always be rigorous about:

- Keeping each element of each slide (header, footer, text box) in the same spot
- Including slide numbers
- Standardizing font sizes (this will keep you honest about concision, too)
- Maintaining a consistent margin.

Keep it simple: Every slide should be easy to read, with a clearly recognizable key point. No one wants to have to spend time puzzling over a visual. When your audience can recognize your point easily, they'll also be more likely to retain that information. And if the audience has to struggle to interpret the slide, guess what they are NOT doing at that moment. Listening to you.

Find a proofreader: Ask a colleague to read your slides. Everyone needs an editor to point out spelling errors, missing words, or a confusing sentence.

Use variety: No, I'm not contradicting myself. Within a consistent overall deck, you can still find ways to use a variety of layouts to create visual interest. When people see the same format—three bullet points on the left, an image on the right—over several slides, they might start to glaze over. Using a few variations helps keep your audience interested. Color, too, can be an easy way to add visual interest to your slides, whether it is pops of color at key points or a change in background color to amplify the message of a particular slide. Just be aware of any meaning behind certain colors (such as the positive/negative connotation of green/red, which can change depending on where you are in the world).

Simple can be better than stylish: We all have access to ever more esoteric ways of presenting data—and bar graphs can look old-fashioned next to radar charts. But if a bar graph more clearly illustrates the point you are trying to make, it makes more sense to be plain and effective than flashy and confusing.

Try animations (cautiously): Animations can be useful in isolating visual elements—bringing in one bullet point at a time, for instance. But be careful not to get too elaborate; stick to the fastest fade setting.

Know your audience: If you know you're presenting to an executive who is a stickler for the company templates, make sure you have the right one, and that the template colors and fonts are consistent throughout. Don't give your audience a reason to discount your credibility.

Email (and other business writing)

Obviously, slide decks are not the only written communication we rely on in our professional lives. Other types of business writing, especially email, comprise a big chunk of the way we get across our ideas or ask for action.

Whole books have been written about email or business writing. I'm not going to tackle the techniques and tools specific to successful persuasive writing here. But, if you've been paying attention to the rest of this book, you'll know that there's one underlying principle behind all communication. It's about connection, and to connect you need to think about your audience. How are they reading your communication? How easily can they find the key point, the action item, or the ask? When does the email hit their inbox? These questions can guide the way you compose your email.

For instance, a large percentage of emails get opened and read on a mobile device. But where do we typically write emails? On a computer, with a big monitor. So what we as writers see is a large window, in which a chunk of text doesn't look overwhelming. But when that long paragraph arrives on a mobile screen, it suddenly feels like a tome. If you've listed two or three questions or action items toward the end of your email, chances are you will only get a response to the first one—because your reader has scrolled to the first question she sees and hit "reply."

So when you sit down to write that email or pre-read document, think about your audience.

Where will they read it? You may not be able to answer this question definitively, but if you have any doubt, make sure that even someone reading on a phone will get the key points. Put your ask or reason for writing in the first line. Craft a descriptive, meaningful subject line.

Who needs to read it? If you need someone to read the email, make sure they are in the to: line, not cc. Because of the massive overflow of email that bombards us all, many executives have adopted an email-sorting rule that sends any email in which their name doesn't appear in the to: line to a separate folder. Odds are that folder isn't opened up very often.

On the flip side, make sure that everyone on the email really *needs* to be on the email. Nobody wants extraneous messages clogging up their inbox.

When should they read it? Receiving an email on a Saturday has a very different impact than receiving one on a Tuesday. Just the appearance of an email over the weekend gives it an aura of urgency that may not be deserved. If you are working on email over the weekend but the messages don't need to be dealt with until the workweek starts, just save it in drafts and hit send first thing on Monday.

Finding the Right Way to Connect

Not long ago, I made a decision about a key benefits program for our company. I was excited about it; I felt like I was making a good call for the whole team. That Friday afternoon, pumped up, I sent out a Slack message to everyone announcing the big news. I was surprised when not a single person responded to it.

A few days later, I asked one of my colleagues about it. "Why didn't anybody respond?"

She laughed and told me, "Dean, it was a lot to take in right before the weekend. And it wasn't really an announcement that works well on Slack—you would have been better off sending an email."

It's a mistake almost everyone has made at one time or another—sending an instant message when an email would better convey the information, sending an email instead of communicating face-to-face. We're all multitasking and trying to check off items on our to-do list but spending thirty seconds evaluating a few factors will help you avoid sending the wrong message or irritating the person you are communicating with.

How complex is the information you are conveying? Anything that requires more than a few words to explain, or that contains multiple layers of information, should be sent as an email. Simpler requests or notes might be better suited to casual conversations over IM.

How quickly do you need a response—or, how invasive are you willing to be? Slack or other instant messaging tools and texting are made for quick-fire, rapid-response situations. Email is more likely to sit in an inbox for a few hours. Of course, these days an unscheduled phone call signals its own kind of urgency. Evaluate whether you need to grab someone's attention right away and potentially interrupt them in the midst of a task or meeting, or if it can wait for a more opportune time.

How sensitive is the subject? If you need to communicate something that will impact someone's day-to-day, or that might meet with resistance, consider doing it face-to-face, or at least over the phone. This also shows respect for your audience.

How important is tone? Nuances are often lost with the written word. Emoticons can ease some of this loss of affect but aren't always appropriate for an office. If you have any doubt that you can convey the right tone in writing, do it over the phone or in person.

When are you communicating? Is it business hours, early morning or evening, or over the weekend? This is where setting expectations for your team is key. Do you want your team to be on call at all times? If that's your business environment, perhaps texting or IM at all hours is okay (whether this is healthy or good for business in the long-term is another discussion). But for most, IM should be saved for in-business hours.

What about email? Again, it's best to set expectations ahead of time. I might send an email over the weekend because I've found a few hours to knock out my to-do list, but I don't expect my team to be checking in or responding to emails until the workweek begins. Other managers want their team to respond to requests in off-hours, but without the house-on-fire urgency of texting or IM. With expectations in place, team members can then take responsibility for how they handle email: constantly checking or setting aside an hour or two to deal with work requests.

When and how we communicate sends its own message; how quickly we need a response, how sensitive the topic might be, how much we've thought about our audience and their reception of the material. By putting a few extra seconds into considering the tool and the timing, we can increase our odds of communicating successfully.

Speaking Up

Brian had all the qualities of a great speaker. He enunciated clearly, projected to the back of the room, paused appropriately. He made eye contact around the room, used his body language effectively, and exuded charisma. But when it came to message, he failed to make any key points, and his overall goal and ask were often unclear. People usually left the room wondering what he was getting at, why they were in the room, or how this could possibly be relevant to them. He was charming and engaging, but he lost opportunity after opportunity because he couldn't articulate his goal or ask directly for the resource he sought. Despite all his natural speaking gifts, Brian wasn't a great communicator.

*

Sandra always made sure she was well prepared before she approached any communication opportunity. She did her research, identified her goal, organized her key points, and aligned her ask with the needs and concerns of her audience. She thought through every detail and her story clearly was a direct appeal to the individuals in the room.

Sandra's message was on point. But when she stood up to speak, her nerves always got the better of her. Even before she began speaking, she could barely catch her breath and her hands began shaking. Her sentences were plagued with verbal pauses and filler words, she rarely made eye contact, and she rocked back and forth and fidgeted nervously with the clicker. Everyone could see how panicked she felt. Eager to sit back down, she raced through her content so quickly that no one was able to absorb what she was saying. Sandra's carefully prepared message went unheard.

*

Delivery *does not* exist in isolation—but it *is* an important differentiator. As Brian demonstrates, you can have great stage presence—and no substance. Great delivery impresses if, and only if, the substance of the message is strong. Style without substance might carry you for a while, but intelligent and well-informed audiences will quickly see through the charade. For Brian, *preparation* is key: understanding his audience and honing his message.

Sandra, on the other hand, is an example of someone so overwhelmed by nerves that all the message preparation in the world is not enough. For Sandra, *practice* becomes essential: running through her presentation, out loud, and understanding methods to calm her nerves.

Great delivery is based on two things: connection and confidence. Sometimes we convince ourselves that confidence and an ability to connect with others are qualities you are either born with, or not. People say: "I'm just not a good public speaker. My nerves get the best of me." Or: "I can't be myself when I'm speaking, because I've been told that my natural demeanor is wrong."

But, like any skill, cultivating great delivery is a matter of practice, preparation, and persistence.

First, you need to build on the skills we've already developed. After all, the entire model has been constructed deliberately to boost both your confidence and delivery, simply by following a simple path:

Let Go of the Messenger Mindset (chapter 1): Speak as a visionary; rather than telling people where they are, tell them where to go

The Persuasion Challenge (chapter 2): Be aware of the context in which you are speaking

Assess (chapter 3): Know your goals and your audience

Message (chapter 4): Craft a persuasive and memorable message

Document (chapter 5): Create a simple and clear slide deck or other visual support

With these tools, you can stand in front of an audience and demonstrate conviction in your message and confidence in yourself. In turn, you will appear more credible, and your message will be more persuasive and compelling.

Of course, not everyone sets out to inspire hundreds of employees or command a room full of executive leaders. Some of us just want to communicate clearly with a team of colleagues or reports.

In either case, the key is to eliminate the distractions that stem from either poor message preparation or fear and anxiety around public speaking. Once these distractions have been eliminated, you can begin to add in strengths. Eventually, the path opens up beyond delivery to executive presence: the combination of confidence, authority, and competence that distinguishes corporate leaders. (For a checklist to help guide you through, please see the appendix: "Deliver Effectiveness Review.")

Let's start with the basics: how to communicate in a clear, uncluttered way that allows your persuasive message to shine through. Then we'll turn to cultivating executive presence.

Eliminating Distractions, Adding Value

When you stand up in front of a room to speak, do you feel a flush of heat, a shaky energy? Are your thoughts racing? Most of us feel something like this, because public speaking initiates a primal physiological response: fight or flight. Those surges of energy come from adrenaline coursing through your body. Once you understand what's going on, you can turn this energy into power, rather than letting it overwhelm you. You just need to practice how to respond to it, how to reduce the appearance of nerves, and release enough of the tension ahead of speaking so that you can control your voice, your body language, and your connection to the audience.

I've heard a similar story about a well-known basketball player. He told coaches in high school that, when called upon to take last-minute free throws when the game was on the line, he felt "butterflies." At one point a coach told him, "Hey, everybody feels butterflies; that's just being human. The idea is to figure out how to make those butterflies fly in formation." The point is, we get nervous because it is a natural human reaction to a stressful situation. When you can shift from pushing that feeling away to acknowledging it and harnessing its energy, the butterflies can actually help you give your best performance.

At base, delivery should be about conveying your message in a way that doesn't distract and that allows your key points to be heard. Many of us know generally what might be distracting—"ums" and "ahs" are a universal plague—but we don't spend much time thinking about how to reduce these tics. The key is awareness and practice. When we know that we are making these mistakes, we can begin to be aware of every time we use them.

Verbal pauses (um, ah) and filler words (like, so, OK, you know): Most of us fall back on verbal pauses in our speech, even when we aren't particularly nervous. When I first started to speak in public, I had tons of confidence, but I also used tons of "ums" and "ahs." I had no idea how often I used these verbal pauses—I didn't hear myself saying them. So I started recording myself. Reviewing my speech this way made me much more aware of these verbal tics, and I began to use them less and less. It's not a quick process—it took me a year to eliminate this habit. But it's well worth the effort, because all those "ums," "ahs," and "you knows" are a big distraction and can make you sound less professional.

Self-reflection—figuring out *why* you use verbal pauses or filler words—can help you reduce the frequency with which they appear in your speech. Sometimes we try to command ourselves to make a change: "I've got to stop using um and ah!" But this often has the opposite effect: we become so nervous about using these words that we use them more.

Consider possible reasons for using pauses or filler words:

> You can't think of what you want to say next or you're uncomfortable with silence. ("Umm...")
> You need a segue or a transition between sentences or thoughts ("like...," "so...")
> You want to reassure yourself that the audience is following you ("right?...," "okay?..." "you know?...")

By listening back to your recorded conversations (even casual phone calls can be instructive), you can begin to understand why you use the words and start to practice eliminating them. As you determine why you are using these words, you can find ways to reduce their appearance by practicing out loud more often, sharpening your transitions, and finding other techniques to engage with your audience.

Weak, qualifying language (kind of, a little bit, basically): We sometimes feel the need to soften our observations or recommendations: "This is a solution, kind of…" "Our solution, I think, is to…" Does this telegraph confidence? Of course not. Many of us want to avoid sounding aggressive or prescriptive, appear inclusive of the audience, or justify our recommendation. If you're unsure which undermining phrases you use, ask a colleague to listen to you speak and note them for you. We're often unaware of how frequently we use these terms.

But if you listen to experts speak in their fields, you'll notice that they make declarative statements. They don't justify or undermine their idea. If you have the clarity of message and the business case to back up your recommendation, it's not belligerent to say so. A strong, direct, purposeful statement, in fact, is more likely to induce agreement.

Fidgeting or rocking: Some communication experts caution against certain habits such as walking around the stage, perhaps, or putting your hands in your pockets. I disagree. If it is natural to you to walk from one side of the stage to the other, go for it; just make sure it doesn't distract from the substance of what you are saying. If you feel comfortable with one hand in your pocket, go for it—just don't jiggle your keys. Be cognizant of the context. If you're in an informal environment, a hand in the pocket can signal that you're relaxed and comfortable. If you're speaking to a team of executives, it can appear unpolished.

However, certain movements betray your nerves—things like repetitive rocking on your feet, fidgeting with the clicker or your papers, tapping your hand on your leg, or tapping your foot against the floor. And once your audience notices it, that's all they'll notice.

Lack of eye contact: You cannot connect with your audience if you don't look at them. When you don't make eye contact, you seem less confident, your communication seems less authoritative, and your credibility diminishes. In a small group, make sure you make individual eye contact, lingering just long enough to let each person know you are speaking directly to them. It's a subtle art to linger long enough without making someone feel uncomfortable but when you get the timing right, it is powerful.

Make sure you understand the cultural context, though. In the United States, eye contact denotes confidence and respect. However, in other countries (many areas in Asia, for instance), eye contact might indicate aggression or rudeness. If you've done your pre-work of assessing the audience, you can calibrate your eye contact to local expectations.

Dependence on notes: The problem here is threefold. First, if you are reading off notes or slides, you aren't making eye contact. Second, being wedded to your notes makes it more likely that you might get flustered by a question or by losing your place. Third, a dependence on notes generally means you've constructed a monologue—and true communication always needs to have the possibility of dialogue.

If you're the type of person who likes to prepare by writing a script in advance, go ahead and do it. But over time, whittle your script down to an outline, and from an outline to bullet points. Don't try to memorize the presentation verbatim, but practice thinking of the key points you need to cover on each slide or at each stage. These simple bullet points will jog your memory and enable you to recall what detail you need to add at each point in the presentation.

Reliance on jargon: Jargon is the junk food of language. Like a drive-thru hamburger, jargon is filling but void of value, because it lacks the specificity that would give it real meaning. Expressions like baked in, deep dive, low-hanging fruit, in the cards, outside the box, pass the smell test, gain traction, etc., can make you sound unprepared or lazy in your thinking. Rather than a shortcut to the association you intend, they can alienate or annoy audiences.

The best way to handle nearly all of these distractions is to practice, practice, practice. Practicing out loud lets us feel looser, more confident, and reinforces the message in our own mind, making it easier to communicate to others.

In addition to practicing out loud in your office, in the car, in front of a mirror, or with a colleague, it can be particularly helpful to practice out loud just before speaking. Taking a moment out in the hallway to go through the first minute of your presentation allows that first, most powerful flush of adrenaline to run its course. I think of it as a warm-up before a workout.

Once you've tackled the distractions you want to reduce, you can begin to think about the strengths that will add conviction, value, and inspiration to your delivery. A common adage proposes, "It's not what you say, it's how you say it." I believe it should be "It is both what you say AND how you say it."

First and foremost—**be appropriate.** Do I want you to be authentic? Yes. But that doesn't mean being yourself at the expense of the context and the audience. With every one of the points that follow, ask yourself: am I behaving in a way that is appropriate for my subject, for the venue, and for the audience to whom I am speaking?

The "What":

Use storytelling: A personal story or illustrative example captures attention, builds a sense of connection, and can be more memorable than a simple recitation of facts.

Use rhetorical devices to break up the content and highlight important information: Ask real or rhetorical questions. Use internal summaries to remind your audience of the main issues. Speak in bullet points and use verbal highlights ("The key point here is...," "This is important because...") to draw attention to essential information and encourage note-taking. Pause and repeat information you want your audience to absorb.

Keep your sentences short and simple: Use periods, not commas. When listeners have to parse complicated sentence structure, they'll lose track of your point. Of course, you don't want every sentence to be a simple noun-verb-subject, but your key points should be.

Include What's In It For You (WIIFY) statements: Connect what you are saying directly and specifically to your audience.

Deploy humor: A joke can help set the room at ease and foster a positive connection between you and the audience. However, pay close attention to what is appropriate for your environment and audience. Nothing is worse than a joke that falls flat or offends someone.

The "How":

Develop compelling body language: Use your hands to gesture at key points. Move deliberately through your space. Maintain eye contact (in a culturally appropriate way). Engage briefly with your slides but return to the audience.

Focus on tone, pacing, and volume: Use the appropriate energy—smile and be enthusiastic if you are making a pitch for a new program; take a more serious tone when it is a "bad news" presentation. Pause at key moments to let your audience digest what you tell them. Don't race through your content. Make sure everyone in the room can hear you. Vary your tone; give emphasis to your key points.

Begin and end with confidence: Starting with a warm, engaging introduction and ending with a polished, assured sign-off demonstrates your confidence, establishes your credibility, and leaves your audience with a final positive impression.

Use strong vocabulary: Show your confidence in your message by including strong action words such as deliver, direct, exceed, generate, influence, initiate, integrate, leverage, maximize, structure.

Some of this comes down to practice, too. But in large part, strengths are added to your delivery skills through preparation—taking the time to think through your audience and your message and including appropriate techniques and language in your speaking toolbox.

Five Traits of Strong Delivery

A speaker who delivers her persuasive message well usually hits five key markers. A great speaker will:

Capture Attention: Through body language, tone and pace, storytelling, and audience involvement.

Maximize Retention: Through storytelling, specific examples, and individual callouts ("Jim, this point is important to you...").

Show Confidence: With body language, tone and pace, and strong vocabulary.

Create Connection with the Audience: Through storytelling, rhetorical devices, humor, and a warm opening and polished sign-off.

Create Connection between the Content and the Audience: Using real examples, references to their priorities, tone and pacing, individual callouts, and WIIFY statements.

Handling Your Nerves

Glossophobia (the fear of public speaking) is real and affects a wide swath of the population to one degree or another. But we aren't all doomed to break out in a sweat every time we have to speak in front of an audience. I have my own "tell" when I get nervous, but over the years I've found ways to deal with it.

I tend to be very anxious. With anxiety, everything is super sped up and I can't remember what I said a minute ago. When I'm calm, everything slows down and I'm much better able to think things through. Every workshop, I take a few minutes before class starts to re-center myself.

It strikes some people as counterintuitive, but I find it crucial to practice but NOT to memorize. When you memorize everything you want to say, you may sound polished, but it impedes the primary goal of communication: connection. If you simply read a script, you are no longer engaged with your audience, there's no chance for dialogue, and if you get interrupted or you lose your place, suddenly the whole presentation gets derailed. And that's uncomfortable for everyone.

Listen for Better Delivery

We've discussed the importance of active listening in becoming an excellent communicator, as it helps you gather important information in the process of bringing together a message that resonates with your audience. But you can also use listening while you are speaking to refine and enhance your message and encourage your audience to listen as well.

Once you are in the meeting or on the phone call, use the following strategies to both gather new information and incorporate it into your presentation:

> **Collect:** Have a game plan for how you will elicit new information. Will you try to build in five minutes at the beginning for introductions and small talk? Are

you going to ask questions of your audience as you speak? Collecting information on the spot makes it more likely that you'll hear what's happening right now in your audience's mind. Cultivate your active listening skills. (See chapter 3 if you need a refresher.)

Reflect: Now that you have some new information, think about how to incorporate it into your speech. Refer back to an anecdote someone shared in the beginning or address a concern someone brings up. Saying something like, "Jim, you told me that..." will make your audience feel listened to, demonstrate your respect for their words, and make them pay closer attention to what you have to say. (There's nothing like hearing your own name to make you sit up and focus in a meeting. It may sound simplistic, but it is powerful.)

How to Deliver Detail

We live in an age of information; constant, engulfing, overwhelming information. And in opposition, our attention spans grow ever shorter and our ability to listen carefully erodes by the day.

In this reality, being able to gauge the *right amount* of detail is crucial. After all, we need detail to give specificity to our message, to provide support to our argument, and to capture attention. But we need to interrogate every detail that goes into our persuasive communication.

The first question: What detail does our audience want or need?

Second: What detail is crucial to understand our message?

Third: How are we presenting our detail, so that it is easy to understand and remember?

The answers to these three questions inform the way we approach our message, as we think about key themes (which can often be expressed as chapters). If we set out our message clearly, our audience should understand what the key themes are from the beginning, and the details clearly fall under specific themes.

But our delivery is also a key element in communicating detail clearly, concisely, and memorably. Techniques such as internal summary, repetition of key points, and pausing allow your audience to absorb the detail you've designated as important.

Rhetorical cues, such as bullet-point lists ("I want you to remember three things: 1...2...3...") and WIIFY statements ("This is important to you because..." or "This is what you need to remember..."), work as verbal highlighters for the listener. These kinds of cues often compel listeners to pick up their pens to take notes.

Delivering detail in the right way, at the right time, allows us to bolster our argument or paint a memorable picture without losing our audience.

Hit Record!

When you set out to eliminate bad delivery habits or cultivate good new ones, there's one tool that beats any other for effectiveness (even as it makes everyone squirm): video recording.

When you record yourself speaking, there's no hiding your weak spots. Video forces you to notice how many verbal pauses infiltrate your speech, how often you rock back and forth on your heels, or if you look at your slides more than your audience.

Another tip: put it on fast-forward. This lets you focus only on body language, while making exaggerated or distracting motions very noticeable.

Finally, get a colleague to watch you or watch the recording and give you constructive feedback. Sometimes we don't see a habit as something distracting, but a peer can call out how many times you say "So" as you transition from slide to slide.

POWERFUL DELIVERY, REMOTELY

Business reality these days dictates that you aren't always in the same room with your audience. Companies are global, with teams in different time zones; employees work remotely or on flexible schedules; getting everyone into a room together can be impossible. How do you convey a powerful presence when you are running a conference call or a virtual meeting?

It's hard enough to maintain someone's attention when you are in the same room; when we're connected only by phone or computer, the hurdles to capturing attention are even higher. We've likely all had the unsettling feeling during a virtual meeting that no one is on the other end of the line or have asked a question in that situation and been met with what feels like an ocean of silence.

So how do you make sure that other people *are* listening and engaged when you are in charge of a virtual meeting?

In some ways, the same basic principles of persuasive communication apply. Hone your message to a strong, direct statement. Know your audience: what you need them to know, and what they want to know. Make sure the information you present to them is easy to follow, and that you emphasize your key points.

But delivering information over the phone or video has its own unique challenges, and its own unique solutions. The following techniques can help you grab your audience's attention, keep them engaged, and pull them back when they get distracted (and they will). For those managing remote teams, keeping everyone focused and aligned is of particular concern, and making the most of every communication opportunity is key. Consider the following techniques:

Meeting Management

- **Set the ground rules:** Let all the attendees know your expectations, and that you may call on them at times. Set out a meaningful objective: "We're here for the next thirty minutes—let's agree to stay present and work efficiently so that we maximize the time." Most people will read between the lines: don't multitask!

- **Spread the responsibility:** Have team members take on a section of the meeting by giving an update on a project or an aspect of an ongoing initiative. Changing the voice will capture everyone's attention and get people used to contributing.

- **Stay focused on the call:** Designate someone else to manage the chat feature when you are running a WebEx. That person can draw your attention to particularly relevant questions, which you can then read aloud to the entire group and answer verbally.

- **Be a tough cop:** If things start to veer off course, be assertive about keeping things to the stated agenda. And police yourself most of all: don't start digressing as the leader of the conversation. Stay focused on your message.

- **End on time:** Or early! Stay on task, so that you can wrap up well within your stated time frame. No one ever wants a meeting to go late, especially when they have a full slate of other meetings that fills the rest of their day. Give everyone a chance to absorb the information you've imparted, and allow people to clear their heads for the next task to come.

Audience Engagement

- **Make it visual:** Whenever possible, use videoconferencing. Being able to see each other not only forges stronger bonds, it helps people stay focused on the task at hand. When everyone is visible, the team leader can spot when someone drifts off, and bring them back into focus on the task at hand.

- **Repeat:** As speakers, it's natural to worry about boring your audience by saying the same thing over and over. But here's the key: in any presentation, and especially in a remote presentation, any given audience member is going to miss a significant percentage of what you say. An email comes in, a colleague drops by, another meeting is coming up—the ways we can be distracted are endless. If a piece of information is crucial, say it again—and again, and maybe even again. You can acknowledge the repetition, but don't fear it.

- **Cultivate participation:** Ask questions. Tap someone to give a project update. Share your screen and have a team member pull up documents while you continue to run the meeting. Use polling software to keep people engaged and gather data from those less likely to speak up. The more opportunities people have to be active in a remote meeting, the less likely they will be to drift off, check their email, or start preparing for their next meeting.

- **Call on participants by name:** Avoid a general question like "Are there any questions?" or "Does that make sense?" These are easy to avoid, and chances are you'll be met with silence. Instead, ask for feedback from specific individuals, i.e., "Susan, how does that relate to your part of the business?" or "Will, how do you think your team will react to this new deadline?"

- **Plant a participant:** A great way to make sure everyone is paying attention is to encourage participation— comments, questions, conversation. But especially when engaging remotely, people hesitate to break the ice. Try designating a team member ahead of time to comment or ask a question to get things rolling; however, DON'T spring this on someone. You never want to embarrass people by calling them out when they are unprepared.

- **Give your audience time:** Most facilitators wait five to eight seconds for an audience to answer a question before moving on. It's awkward to sit in silence. But when you are on the phone or video, participants might have muted their line or hesitate to be the first one to speak up (see above). You may need to let that silence hang a bit longer to get the response you want.
- **Make it personal:** Add a few minutes in your regular meeting to acknowledge your team members, whether by noting significant work accomplishments, anniversaries, or birthdays.

What about for yourself? Many of the pitfalls that afflict a virtual audience—the ease of multitasking, the lack of personal engagement—can affect a speaker as well. A few techniques can help you keep up your energy and engagement, and demonstrate your leadership, even over a phone line:

- **Stand** to increase your feeling of energy. This will also help with vocal projection, volume, and tone.
- **Smile,** whether your audience can see it or not. Just the action itself can change your tone of voice.
- **Ask** questions; if you set a goal of asking one or two follow-up questions when someone else talks, you'll focus more on listening.
- **Pause and defer** when someone interrupts, rather than speaking over them.

BEYOND DELIVERY: THE ART OF EXECUTIVE PRESENCE

When we talk about delivery at its most inspiring, we often use the phrase "executive presence." What does this term mean? Executive presence is about *communicating* clearly and effectively, *connecting* to people, and demonstrating *confidence* authentically. Executive presence means that not only is your message well crafted, personalized to your audience, and memorable, but that your delivery reinforces and enhances that message. While executive presence can be demonstrated every day, in all of your interactions, behaviors, and decisions, I'll focus here on how it manifests itself through communication, especially more formal speaking opportunities.

Think of executive presence as a building: one that is supported by three pillars. These three pillars are practicable and measurable—which means that executive presence isn't an inherent trait, but a skill that can be honed. As you use The Latimer Group's techniques to bolster your pillars, your building can become more stable and robust. But if any of the pillars are missing or weak, the building is in danger of collapsing.

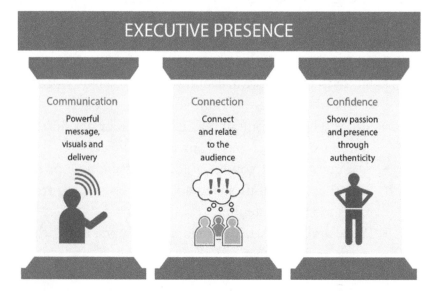

EXECUTIVE PRESENCE

Communication	Connection	Confidence
Powerful message, visuals and delivery	Connect and relate to the audience	Show passion and presence through authenticity

The Three Pillars of Executive Presence depend on all the skills we've practiced prior to standing up and speaking. Communication and Connection have been crucial to shaping your awareness, your message, and your document, while Confidence is built from the hard work you've put into each of those stages, as well as the time you've dedicated to practicing your delivery.

What I've found again and again is that when someone struggles with establishing executive presence, the problem generally lies elsewhere: little understanding of the audience, an unclear goal, or poor story construction. As you work to cultivate executive presence, first make sure that you've followed the Latimer Model: from Assess to Message to Document. Once you're confident that you have a basic understanding of your audience and their context, have crafted a clear goal and a set of strong key points to get you there, and have documented your presentation appropriately, you can begin to think about ways to project confidence and authenticity, conviction and expertise, leadership and motivation.

Keep in mind that executive presence isn't just about what you say; it's how you say it, what expression you have on your face, what kind of energy you project, where you stand in the room, and how you engage with your audience.

And a persuasive, compelling presence also doesn't start when you stand up to speak. It begins when you enter the room—whether you are fidgeting or biting your nails before you go on, if you have your head down, if you are squinting or grimacing. People notice these tiny details, and it affects how they receive you once you do begin to communicate.

According to research conducted by economist Sylvia Ann Hewlett, executive presence is comprised of gravitas, communication, and appearance. "It's an amalgam of qualities that telegraphs that you are in charge or deserve to be," Hewlett writes in her book, *Executive Presence.* Our approach to presence enables you to develop deeper self-awareness and provides practical tools to help you prepare so that when you stand in front of an audience, you can do so with confidence. That assurance, along with our techniques for strengthening each pillar, will help you communicate at the highest level.

Albert's greatest weakness was apparent from the moment he introduced himself in the Executive Presence workshop. He spoke quickly and indistinctly, slurring his words together. His voice was soft, and he barely took a breath from sentence to sentence. I had to focus intently on him in order to understand what he was saying.

In his first presentation, Albert's rapid pace and soft-spoken tone persisted. In his opening, he asked a question of the audience—but no one was sure enough of what he'd said to respond. As he continued through his key points, the audience struggled to maintain attention.

In my feedback, I emphasized the importance of clarity and enunciation in creating a sense of connection with both a speaker and his or her message. We also discussed the importance of using storytelling to demonstrate both vulnerability and authenticity.

In his second presentation, Albert took all these notes seriously. He opened with a story that demonstrated how we all determine our brand loyalty and told a self-deprecating joke about his dependence on caffeine. The audience relaxed, and with their attention captured, were more receptive to the key message Albert then delivered.

Crucially, by being open and vulnerable, Albert allowed himself to be authentic, which then also made it easier for him to speak more loudly, deliberately, and clearly. This time, when he asked his question, everyone in the audience could answer. The audience didn't have to listen as intently to understand what he was saying—but they wanted to listen intently to his content, because they felt a connection to Albert and a connection to his passion for the topic.

Albert's transformation demonstrated something remarkable about executive presence: how rapidly dramatic progress can be made, just by taking some risks, becoming more self-aware, and allowing yourself to be authentic.

THE THREE PILLARS OF EXECUTIVE PRESENCE

The First Pillar: Communication

This pillar rests directly on having spent time determining a clear, powerful message. Now, make sure you know your message—your goal, the key points, and the potential objections—cold. Any hesitation or confusion will undermine your confidence. And don't rely on your slide deck to be your script. The audience can read your slides for themselves. Your job is to tell them what the slide means.

Consider how the delivery of your message allows your audience to understand, care about, and act on the topic you are speaking about. Speak clearly and succinctly, highlight the key points, and connect them to your audience. Be sure that your clear communication is easy to follow, provides ways for the audience to process or consume your message, and includes memorable points that will stick with the audience for long-term retention.

The Second Pillar: Connection

Again, there is no second pillar without the work you've already done to understand your audience. Once you've laid that foundation, use strong, vivid language that is collaborative and inclusive; take a confident stance that faces the audience directly and openly; tailor the tone of your voice to your message.

Choose anecdotes and examples that speak to your audience's priorities and concerns. Storytelling can be an amazingly effective technique for confident, persuasive communication. Anecdotes and examples bring an argument to life and create a memorable sense of personality and engagement. In the right context, vulnerability can paradoxically show your power and confidence.

Think carefully about your first impression. A warm greeting, a smile, and a genuine interest in the people you speak with can set the tone immediately. Make sure to introduce yourself and learn everyone's name in the room; demonstrating your appreciation for your audience will create an atmosphere of respect.

Everyone knows that eye contact is important, but few do it really well—it's hard to look people in the eye with conviction while also focusing on hitting all your key points and thinking on your feet. Like anything, this is a skill that requires practice.

Even small gestures can create a feeling of connection and thoughtfulness: using "we" instead of "I"; avoiding exclusionary terms like "guys"; using individual callouts to speak to particular audience members.

The Third Pillar: Confidence

Even if you feel confident, you may still be stuck in habits that make you appear nervous or hesitant. Again, make sure that you make consistent eye contact with the entire room; square your shoulders to the room (don't try to hide by standing sideways!); use a forceful, varied speech pattern that appropriately emphasizes your key points; and willingly engage with questions and dialogue, even skeptical or critical dialogue.

Give yourself the opportunity to get into the right mindset. Amy Cuddy popularized the idea of "power posing"—using purposeful movement and poses to affect how you feel (and how others then perceive you). This notion has drawn its fair share of critics—but my experience has shown that following some kind of ritual before you stand up to speak, be it power posing, meditating, taking a walk, or talking through your key points, helps put you in a frame of mind that is calmer, more confident, and better prepared to communicate effectively.

Demonstrating confidence and authority can take many forms. In addition to using powerful body language, use powerful verbal language: strong active verbs, few hesitations or filler words, short declarative sentences. Use your authority to keep control of the room: don't hesitate to interrupt if digressions or questions are running on too long. Project your voice to every corner of the room, and ask questions.

Key Qualities of Executive Presence

Be aware: Know yourself and know your audience. Spend time in your assessment phase figuring out your strengths and weaknesses in this particular situation, and the specific needs and wants of your audience.

Be present: Give the moment your full attention. Turn off your phone. Shut down your email. This singular focus has become so unusual that this alone will help you stand out.

Be inclusive: Recognize your biases, use "we" language, and show your respect for your audience.

Be vulnerable: Be willing to make a more personal connection through stories.

Be adaptable: Stay alert to your audience and their reactions. Take nonverbal cues as seriously as verbal ones and change course if you sense the mood shifting to a negative one.

Creating the Connection

Why do we communicate? Why is it important to communicate well?

I believe that there is a very simple, very profound answer to this question: connection.

> *After fifteen years of social work education, I was sure of one thing: Connection is why we're here; it is what gives purpose and meaning to our lives.*
> *– Brené Brown*

Communication is the way that we, as humans, connect to other humans. Persuasive communication transcends the simple transmission of information from one person to another; rather, it forges interpersonal bonds, which—yes—help us achieve our objective, but also build relationships.

Successful communication requires that we approach our fellow humans with *curiosity* (a desire to learn about them, their context, and their culture); with *empathy* (demonstrating respect and seeking common ground); and with *exchange* (building dialogue across differences while conveying our own confidence and conviction). Each of these elements lays the foundation for strong, genuine connection.

In this chapter, we'll discuss how to take a purposeful, outcome-oriented approach to cultivating curiosity, empathy, and exchange, and to forging strong connections. And those connections will help us to achieve our ultimate goal: to inspire action.

The Most Important Thing To Know About This Chapter

This is a chapter about entry points, not stopping points.

When I talk about "knowing your audience," about differences in gender, culture, educational background, or generation, I am not advocating judgments, stereotypes, or absolutist thinking. Research is a tool, not a weapon.

I want you to see knowledge as a way to open a conversation toward connection, not an excuse to close your mind to finding common ground.

Curiosity: Learning About Your Audience

I was asked to come in to coach a new executive, Doug, at a growing company. He was struggling to make a mark in meetings, and in a fast-paced, fast-growing business, those meetings were the primary way he was being judged on his competence and leadership abilities.

When we first met, it was clear that Doug was a hard worker and good at his job, but that he was struggling to project that ability to those around him. I asked him to tell me about the next meeting he planned to run, and how that meeting fit into his big-picture goals.

After Doug talked about the message he wanted to convey and the action he hoped to inspire, we turned to the audience. We went through every person who planned to attend: his or her role, how long he or she had been at the company, and to whom he or she reported. We thought about each person's priorities and potential objections to Doug's proposed changes to the business unit.

Doug left our coaching session feeling much more confident about his next meeting. Later he reported that the room felt more receptive to his plan, and that he'd had several productive follow-up conversations. By taking even a few minutes to think more about his audience, he was able to pitch his message directly to the people in the room and make them feel inspired. He looked more authoritative and confident. He connected more clearly with everyone in the room, and they felt more comfortable following his lead.

With a little time and research, we can gather some basic facts about our audience. These allow us to make some intelligent inferences and come up with more insightful questions than we might otherwise devise. Of course, we can't know everything about everyone we set out to communicate with. When we do find out something about a person, we have to be careful to recognize that it is only a small piece of who they are; we need to avoid stereotypes or pre-judgment. But being prepared gives us direction, a generalized understanding of our audience, and a place to begin to learn more about the individuals with whom we want to connect.

As always, this comes with a word of caution:

- Don't make hard judgments.
- Be aware that generalizations and inferences will miss the nuances and specifics of each individual.
- Approach this with a curious, open mind.
- Be aware of the line between being prepared and being *too* knowledgeable. Don't bring in intimate details of someone's personal life. Stay professional and stick to what you know about their work.
- Above all else, use this as a way to *listen* and *connect*.

Bearing these caveats in mind, when you know someone's education, her experience in the company, and her functional area, you can infer, broadly, what she is listening for and what she is trained to do.

For instance, if you have two senior vice presidents in the room, the same age, gender, and tenure at the company, but one is in HR and one is in finance, you can reasonably guess that the VP of HR is going to be listening for something different than the VP of Finance.

What if you notice someone has only been at the company for a year, but he has a PhD? It might make you careful not to treat him as a neophyte, because while he hasn't been working long outside academia, he's certainly accumulated knowledge and expertise in his field.

What guesses might you make about roles?

- Accountant: he listens for solid, informative numbers.
- Operations: she wants to know the product delivery plan.
- Lawyer: she's focusing on who is accountable, and on areas of liability.
- Sales: he's interested in the metrics—what's the potential performance?

It's important to be prepared for a range of different attitudes. If an employee has an associate degree, for instance, she might have really had to hustle to make her way through the corporate structure. That might make her proud—or she could feel resentful of the hurdles she's faced.

Similarly, someone with thirty years of experience might be a knowledgeable leader, ready to guide you to the appropriate resources. Or he might be worn out, jaded, and on the glide path to retirement. The key is to use your knowledge to orient you, but to be prepared for the route to change.

Think about things like military background. A veteran of the armed services is much more likely to want a detailed plan that explores all the contingencies, to be highly organized and structured, and to want to move within the chain of command.

Gathering a minimum of information can help guide us to create a message that resonates with our audience, devise a listening plan that will help us gather even more information, and set out solid starting points in creating a connection between speaker and audience.

CASE STUDY: Alex
Customizing your communication for more effective connection

In goal-oriented communication, few things are more important than creating a sense of connection between yourself and the person you are speaking to. When you are in the audience, what speaker captures your attention more: the one who speaks to your concerns, your needs, and your circumstances, or the one who speaks in generalizations, who addresses broad concerns that may have nothing to do with your situation, and who seems to have little idea who you are or what you might be interested in?

Imagine, for example, that Alex wants to demonstrate the impact of a social media marketing campaign to two audiences. The first audience is an internal team of analysts who want to understand the underlying data and its impact on the company's social capital. The second audience is a room of executives from a client company interested in investing in social media marketing. How will Alex's message—drawing from the same set of data and research—differ?

For the internal team of analysts, Alex delves into the data around click rates and demographics. She digs deep into the details around what exactly made the marketing campaign a success, and how to replicate that success in the future. She puts up spreadsheet after spreadsheet and speaks with expertise about the meaning and significant data points on each.

With her client presentation, Alex instead begins with a powerful story about a single user who engaged with the marketing campaign, and discusses how that user became an influencer who drove many of her friends and family to the service. Her slide deck is simple and clear, bringing forward some of the most significant numbers from the marketing campaign but saving the more detailed spreadsheets in backup for the audience to reference later. Alex connects the specifics of social media use to a broader shift in consumer-to-corporate relationships and uses vivid examples to illustrate her argument. She ties it to the client company's products and demonstrates why this type of social media campaign could be highly successful for their particular needs.

Alex thought about each audience, and their specific objectives. By connecting to what they wanted and needed from the information she was presenting, she was perceived as an expert and a leader both by an audience that craved detail and data, and by an audience that wanted narrative and big-picture analysis.

Bridging a Cultural Divide

People who travel a lot for their jobs usually have a sense of how to integrate themselves into a foreign environment: the polite way to greet a colleague, whether giving or accepting small gifts is customary, a few short phrases in the local language.

But when you are setting out to communicate in a new environment, it is important to think about the small details that might impede or enhance connection. As with understanding your audience's background and context, approach culture with a sense of curiosity: what differences do we have, or what commonalities?

For instance, in the United States we generally associate green with positivity, profits, and go-ahead; red is associated with negativity, losses, and halt. But in China, red is a lucky color and the national color, and drawing a connection that says that red is bad will get you a disgruntled audience.

The differences don't have to cross national boundaries. In the US, an audience in New York and an audience in Arkansas are likely to have as many points of divergence as one in Los Angeles versus one in Moscow. For instance, audiences in the Northeast can be sensitive to gendered language such as "you guys." But in the South, people may scoff at such distinctions. (I had one female client in Tennessee tell me, laughing, "Y'all are really uptight! You've got to let that go.") And the vastness of the US, both in terms of geography and factors such as ethnic and socioeconomic backgrounds, means that any given conference room can hold dramatically different viewpoints and attitudes.

Having some awareness of these areas is useful. However, a sense of curiosity and openness is key, too. You can't know everything about an audience and a culture going in, but you can be willing to cultivate a dialogue and learn.

In addition, you'll want to keep some delivery techniques in mind when you present to an international audience, so that people for whom English is a second language or who don't follow American sports or culture can easily understand and remember the information you are communicating.

Make your references and metaphors universal: If you are on a call with executives from Europe and Asia, telling them that you take a "three yards and a cloud of dust" approach to success (that is, making slow and steady progress) will leave them perplexed. Try a more direct approach—"We focus on pushing hard against obstacles and moving forward with determination."

Keep your sentences simple: In other words, use periods, not commas. Short, "noun-verb-object" sentences make following along and understanding the key point easier for those who are not native speakers of English. (It can help native speakers follow along more easily, too.)

Slow down and pause: Let your audience digest what you give them. Respect the fact that translating your English sentence into their own language (to better understand or remember) might take a moment. Rushing ahead will only cause crucial information to go unheard.

Exchange: Building Dialogue, Confidence, and Authority

Melinda Gates, the well-known philanthropist, once gave an interview to *Fortune* that touched on her investment in VC firms that promote women and minority-led ventures. Gates discussed her role of funding women and supporting women leaders and passed on some advice to women who have a difficult time establishing authority.

> [Interviewer]… when you used to attend meetings with Bill, [you said] people would avoid looking you in the eye or including you in the conversation because they assumed Bill was the decision-maker. What is the best thing for a female founder or VC to do if she finds herself in a similar situation?

> GATES: First of all, she needs to surround herself with people who have her back, who know she is the leader—man or woman. As soon as the person turns to the male at the table, he should reference back to the female founder and say, "Jane actually knows the answer to that. Jane, you and I were just talking about that. Tell them what you think."

> You do that once or twice and the people at the table will stop asking him the questions and realize that she's the one that knows this business deeply, and she's the one who has credibility.

This is fantastic advice. Whether you're a newly emerging leader or an established one who has trouble finding a voice at the table, seek your mentors. Find people who believe in you and be bold; ask them to support you and give you a voice. As you start to demonstrate authority and establish a reputation, consider how you, too, can perpetuate a culture of inclusion. Ask people to speak up. Encourage everyone's voices to be heard.

It will take time, and it's not easy. But communication and leadership—which includes the ability to hear and respect diverse opinions—are inextricably linked. Use both to help your career, develop others, and expand the success of your entire organization.

The Three A's of Exchange

Confident authenticity infuses The Latimer Group approach to delivery. By that we mean that we want you to feel and demonstrate poise, authority, and conviction, while still being true to yourself and your personality.

However, authenticity doesn't mean to speak however you would speak to a friend or family member, whatever the context or the listener. Your authenticity needs to be in balance with what's appropriate to your topic and to your audience.

Think about it as a convergence of three essential qualities:

Authentic: Find a place that feels true and comfortable for you. Don't feel obligated to meet some external ideal of the "perfect speaker." There's no single "right" way to do things—only the right way for you and for your communication.

Agile: Have the flexibility and openness to adjust to new or changing circumstances and audiences. Understanding that speaking to an audience in Beijing is different than speaking to an audience in Boston is just common sense.

Accessible: Meet your audience on common ground. There is a way to stay true to yourself while making yourself easier to understand.

Part of balancing these three attributes is acknowledging and celebrating not only your own authentic self, but that of others—recognizing and respecting differences without ignoring them or running away from them. Be aware of differences in attitudes and perceptions in order to address them as points of division; with knowledge, compassion, and purposeful communication, almost any divide can be bridged.

Jane came to The Latimer Group with a frustrating situation. She was trying to lead a team of younger workers—all millennials—through a leadership program at her company. This program was highly competitive, giving its participants rotational experience through the entire organization. Each year the company would receive more than thirteen hundred applications for only a handful of slots. These were extremely motivated and qualified young people.

Part of the program was to gather periodically as a group for a more generalized classroom-type training. In leading these workshops, Jane noticed that nearly all of the trainees were distracted: openly looking at their phones, talking to each other while Jane was presenting information, even resting their head in their hands and looking out the window. Jane didn't understand. These were superstars, but they were totally unpracticed at concentrating and engaging respectfully during a meeting.

I asked Jane to think about how she structured these meetings. "Well, I start with a PowerPoint on the topic, so that we can work through basic fundamentals of knowledge," she said. "There's Q&A, and then we have a group discussion focused around a specific problem in the field. I've run these kinds of workshops for other workers and they've been successful. I don't understand what's going on here."

I asked her how old the other participants had been, and she thought for a moment. Usually older, she admitted—more likely baby boomers.

I encouraged Jane to think about her goal. What was most important: to train these young men and women in how to behave in a corporate meeting? Or to train them in the material and information she was presenting?

Of course, young workers need to learn how to demonstrate respect to the people who are teaching and guiding them, especially in a technically driven field that requires focus and attention to detail. If you appear to be checked out or uninterested, you won't move far.

But I also advised Jane to think about the particular needs and preferences of her audience. Was there a way to restructure the meeting to make it more interactive? Could the presentation be structured more explicitly as a dialogue, rather than a lecture?

Every audience will have different needs. If we can cultivate our own flexibility, so that we can adapt our communication to best accommodate those needs, our ability to reach and connect will be that much greater.

Finding Common Ground

We all may find ourselves having to confront differences in communication style, preferences, or attitudes. For example, millennials (the largest generation now in the workforce, according to the Pew Research Center) tend to be more digitally adept, more amenable to texting or instant messaging than meetings, and more flexible and open to creative, risky solutions than their older colleagues. These are all differences to be aware of—and to work to connect with—whether you are a baby boomer speaking to a group of millennials, or a millennial leading a team of baby boomers and Gen Xers.

Women can also face differences in communication. For instance, women who are naturally assertive can run into the perception that they are aggressive—and often, men asserting themselves in a similar way are seen as simply confident leaders. Is this fair? Of course not. But it is important to recognize that it does happen and find a way to be strong and powerful without alienating your audience.

On the other hand, women who have a tendency to work communally, to build relationships, and to use stories to cultivate connection can turn these tendencies into powerful leadership qualities. However, they can also be perceived as weaknesses—especially when they aren't accompanied with a confident presence.

And it's also a myth that men can behave as aggressively as they want without consequence. I've worked with male executives who need a coach because their focus on power has led to a failure of communication. Being perceived as combative, pushy, and condescending will disrupt your leadership and communication abilities, whatever your gender.

Gender, generational divides, and diversity in the workplace can be sensitive topics, and there are real issues of discrimination and harassment that require both introspection and concrete action. As society and our understanding of differences continue to evolve, we'll see new issues and points of discussion emerge. However, while recognizing that broad generalizations about people should be approached with caution, I have also seen over many years of coaching that there are discernible differences in communication that are widespread enough to merit discussion. When we approach differences in the workplace with curiosity, exchange, and empathy, we learn from one another and grow as individuals and organizations.

Look Deeper

When you survey a room, you might be tempted to make some assumptions about the diversity of your audience based on appearances. After all, if your audience is of mixed gender and race, it could be tempting to assume that you have a diverse set of viewpoints in the room.

However, if you probe deeper, you might find that the underlying perspectives are more similar than you think. What if all these men and women are of the same generation? What if they all grew up in the same place, went to the same school, studied the same major, and joined the same company around the same time? (I'd say that's quite a coincidence, but bear with me ...) Suddenly, that room is a lot more homogeneous than you would think, because each individual has had very similar formative professional experiences.

Of course, race and gender play a great part in our perspectives and experiences and are important aspects of building a diverse workforce. But in a business setting, understanding the background of our audience—their education and experience—can also have a meaningful bearing on how we communicate successfully with them. When you want to connect with your audience, do the research that gives you information beyond the surface.

And then: *listen.* Make sure that you allow yourself to hear what your audience has to say. Don't discount their perspective because they take a different approach. Be open to a deeper look.

Cultivating Confidence and Conviction

Regardless of gender, race, or generation, anyone who wants to emerge as a leader needs to cultivate confidence and conviction. Cultivating a powerful presence allows you to lead a dialogue, to hear others without diminishing your own natural strengths. We discussed building executive presence in chapter 6, but a few areas are of particular relevance for anyone who steps into a room in which they feel overlooked, underappreciated, or intimidated.

Volume: Do you project your voice and speak loudly enough for others to hear you? Volume shows confidence. Practice projecting your voice so that you can be certain that everyone in the room can hear you.

Tone: Listen to the way you complete your sentences. Do you have a tendency to finish your statements with a rising tone? This up-tone indicates a question, which can undermine your conviction. Be declarative when you finish your sentences. If you have difficulty hearing this in your own speech, record yourself and listen to it. It will take practice to bring your tone down when you finish a sentence.

Word choice: You can reduce your authority by choosing words such as *just, a little,* and *basically,* to describe your work. Take pride in your accomplishments and avoid weak qualifying language that will undermine your credibility.

Hesitation: Be willing to jump in and share your ideas. Anticipate questions so you don't have to pause to consider your answer—any pause allows others to interrupt and take over your discussion.

Being confident in ourselves does not mean diminishing the confidence of others. Demeaning, bullying, or aggressive behavior might get you through a meeting, but in the long run it will work against you. That's where the next element of connection comes in: empathy.

Empathy: Demonstrating Respect and Finding Common Ground

We live in a hyper-charged era, in which people listen less and stake out their beliefs more adamantly than ever before. But if we can approach a room with a willingness to share, to receive, and to connect, we can find common ground and achieve our objectives more easily. True connection requires empathy—a recognition that we are all human, respect for our individuality, a willingness to consider another's perspective, and a willingness to show vulnerability. If we can walk into a room with that attitude, our chances of walking out with an objective met, a successful outcome, or a partnership forged is that much stronger.

The Importance of Respecting Your Audience

Showing your audience respect has a lot of great payoffs—it makes your audience feel engaged and positive; it can enable a culture of buy-in, in which people feel committed not only to execute a plan or implement a new product, but to make it succeed; and it can make you a more engaging, persuasive presenter.

There are a few components to demonstrating respect for your audience.

Listen: Perhaps the most immediate way to show respect for an audience is simply to listen. I've talked about listening a lot throughout the book as a tool to assess and analyze the challenge in front of you, and as a way to be present and connected when you deliver your message. Listening is the most fundamental skill you can have as a speaker; every other skill builds on this one. If you need a refresher, go back to chapter 3 and chapter 6 for more.

Nobody learned anything by hearing themselves speak...You never know what you might learn from simply listening to the people around you...

I sometimes come across people in business, especially if they have been fortunate enough to have some success, that are very fond of their own voices. After saying their piece, they visibly switch off from what others are saying, offering a perfunctory nod or fiddling with their phone, rather than making eye contact and really engaging. Conversely, the most successful entrepreneurs I know all have excellent listening skills in common.

– Richard Branson

Take notes, put away distractions, and ask questions. Really try to understand what you are hearing. Your body language should reflect your commitment to paying attention. And don't forget eye contact—when you feel nervous, it is much easier to look up or down than toward another human being. But this visual connection creates an invaluable bond.

Manage Your Time Wisely: Nearly everyone in every office these days is sprinting constantly. We are all managing too many tasks with too little time. Being cognizant of the demands your audience might have on their time can show both your respect for their mental bandwidth and create a more positive context for your communication.

For example, give your team (and yourself) time between meetings. This lets you all feel less frazzled and more focused, and helps you go into the next meeting clearheaded and refreshed. When you show your team or your clients that you respect their time and their well-being, they will be in a better frame of mind to be persuaded by you.

Once you get into a meeting, make it efficient and well organized. When your audience sees that you respect their time enough to make your points quickly and clearly, they'll respect you more.

In your work, meet your deadlines and arrive on time. Let others know that they can rely on you.

And, finally, be patient. Don't expect things to change overnight. When we try to change our habits, cultivate a new reputation, or effect organizational change, it takes time. Be patient with yourself and others.

Follow the Golden Rule: Pretty simple: treat others like you'd want to be treated.

Be Self-Aware: This one is the inverse of the golden rule: hold yourself to the same standards as you hold others. If you don't follow the same rules and standards you set, your team will notice, and they'll resent it.

Admit when you don't know something: Not only will you learn, but you'll signal that it is okay to ask questions. That helps create a culture of curiosity, honesty, and innovation.

And don't be afraid to be vulnerable; tell a story that connects to a more personal side of your life (remembering to stay on message!). Admit to failure. It may feel like you are opening yourself up to criticism or mockery, but more likely people will admire your courage and relate to you on a human level.

Cultivate Influence: Don't rely on authority to make things happen. When people choose to work with you, want to help you execute your ideas, and feel confident in your ability and expertise, they'll want to help you succeed—and they'll be more likely to go above and beyond what you need from them. When people have to do what you need them to do, because of your title or position, but don't feel influenced by you, there's little incentive to do more than the required work.

Influence and persuasion are close cousins, and when you seek out allies and network, you create a context in which people are more willing to listen to your ideas and more inclined to view them positively. Remember, though, that developing relationships cynically—seeking only to advance your own agenda without thought for what the other person might want or need—will ultimately backfire. Stay connected to your curiosity and to your commitment to exchange.

Respect Both Strengths and Weaknesses: In other words, give others—and yourself—the benefit of the doubt. Not everyone feels comfortable in front of an audience. Try to forgive a misused word or a forgotten data point. If you lose track of your thought in the middle of a sentence, take a pause and start again. Give constructive, thoughtful feedback. If you don't agree with a proposal, or you aren't satisfied with someone's work, take the time to tell people specifically what you think needs to change. A kneejerk reaction of "I don't like this" doesn't help your report or colleague improve, and will create a culture of distrust and fear, which stymies innovation. If people fear being insulted, they'll be less likely to risk proposing something new or distinctive.

Prepare and Follow Through: It's hard to be focused on others when you are feeling unprepared. When you feel anxious because you haven't spent enough time getting comfortable with your material, you'll be too caught up in your own emotions to think about others.

Once your communication is over, make sure that if you say you will do something, you make good on that promise. Nothing conveys respect for your audience like saying directly what you mean and doing what you say you will.

Negotiate: This isn't always easy. Some fear that negotiating or asking an audience for their buy-in will look like weakness. Or they see negotiating as a zero-sum game: the only way I can win is if you lose. But it doesn't have to be that way. The key is in the execution. When done correctly, negotiation will allow your audience to feel good (without requiring you to sacrifice your key points) and create a sense of ownership on both sides.

There are a few important rules to keep in mind when you are negotiating:

Respect your audience: If they react in a way you didn't expect, don't assume that they are ignorant or irrational. Instead, assume that they are being motivated by something you don't yet know, and work to figure it out. Listen to what they have to say and try to understand where they are coming from.

Be willing to give in—but be smart about it: Decide ahead of time what you are willing to give up but go in holding firm to those particular items. As the negotiation proceeds, you can reluctantly give them up—conceding less significant points, without sacrificing your most important goals.

Be strong, but not aggressive: Remember: you might have different goals, but everybody in the room is just trying to get what they need to succeed. Negotiations don't have to be win-or-lose; ideally, every negotiation will be win-win. When the other person walks away feeling good about what happened, they'll be more likely to come in good faith to future meetings.

Do you always want to negotiate? No. Sometimes communication is about delivering an already determined course of action, and persuasion is about making clear the *how* and *why*, not *whether*. But negotiation can be a powerful tool. Used correctly, it can not only help you accomplish your goals, but build your reputation and credibility—and give you even more authority the next time you need to persuade an audience.

Take Care of Yourself: Don't forget: treat *yourself* with kindness and compassion. It's a lot easier to improve if you don't beat yourself up every time you make a mistake or don't perform as well as you'd like. Being kind to yourself becomes easier, too, when you treat others with sympathy and respect—because it becomes easier to believe that your audience isn't judging you harshly if you don't judge others.

Why Connect?

Setting out to make a connection adds a layer of complexity to our preparation; after all, it's a lot easier to just pull together our data, identify some key points, and be able to deliver one presentation to multiple audiences.

But the purpose of communication is, ultimately, connection—even if our harried business environment makes it difficult. If we take a few moments to allow ourselves to be curious, to spark an exchange, and to cultivate empathy, we *will* connect—and that connection makes it more likely that we'll be heard.

Transforming Yourself, Your Organization, and the World

This is a book about creating connection through communication. Every skill we've worked on throughout the book has built on this idea. If you've begun implementing these skills in your own communication, you've seen the difference in the way that people respond to you and the value that you get out of each interaction. Connected, purposeful communication doesn't just achieve the goal of that particular meeting or phone call; it gathers information, and it creates a more responsive, more robust relationship that is mutually beneficial.

Crucially, The Latimer Group doesn't believe that people are either vaguely "good" or "bad" at communication. We believe that ability can be measured and mapped along a spectrum. We know that you can have a strong message but weak slides; great delivery skills but a poorly structured story; beautiful slides but little confidence as a speaker. So The Latimer Group considers very specific elements of each skill as a way to analyze every individual's competency standard and identify precise action items toward improvement. This system of mapping individual skills can in turn be embedded organizationally as part of a communications training curriculum.

The Latimer Model uses metrics to create a well-defined framework for self-improvement and practice. But the beauty of this framework is in its flexibility. You can use it to have better team meetings, conference calls, sales pitches, C-suite presentations, or public speaking engagements. You can use it to refine internal communications, external marketing, or brand ambassadorship. And you can use it to build credibility, foster respect, engage in productive dialogue, and find common ground across political or cultural differences.

Finding Your Level

The Latimer Model evaluates speakers as one of three categories of overall skill: Professional, Leadership, and Executive, across four skills (which we've discussed in chapters 3 through 6): Assess, Message, Document, and Deliver. The key difference is the impact each speaker has on their audience:

> A Professional-level communicator can persuade an audience to **hear** her message (if you've sat through any PowerPoint presentations, you know that just recognizing and remembering the speaker's main point means he or she has done a pretty good job).
>
> A Leadership-level communicator can persuade an audience to **care** about his message.
>
> An Executive-level communicator consistently persuades his audience to **act** on his message.

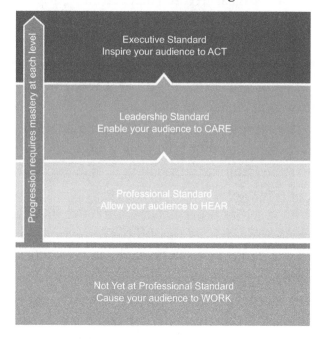

At base, what changes as you move up from level to level is the degree to which people dependably connect to you as a communicator—and the degree to which that connection inspires them to act.

It's important to recognize that an individual can be wonderful at one aspect of presenting and not so great at another. However, these skills are intertwined, and it's very rare to find someone who has Executive-level message skills and Professional (or not yet Professional) delivery skills. Improving in one area will likely improve your skill across all areas. After all, if you feel confident and clear in your message, you'll likely reflect that confidence in the way you speak.

Examining the Levels

When I talk about "hear," "care," or "act," what specific qualities of communication achieve those goals? How does The Latimer Group evaluate a speaker and assign him a level? Here, I'll highlight some of the more important attributes that define each level.

HEAR: "Clarity" and "brevity" define communication at the Professional Standard. The speaker has clarified the message; there are few distractions, and little to get in the way of the message being heard. The message is clear, the slides are relatively simple, and the audience is not overburdened with delivery marred by things like "um, um, um."

CARE: Presenters at the Leadership Standard communicate clearly and create powerful, meaningful audience connection. They identify who the audience is and what is important to them through awareness. They craft a compelling message, tell a story, and convey empathy. Their audience sees the value, understands the context, feels connected, and will remember the key points. The message and the slides make an impact.

ACT: Executive Standard speakers have mastered the ability to communicate a point and the audience feels a strong, meaningful connection. The speakers have command of the situation and the meeting. Most importantly, they are persuasive on a consistent basis across all aspects of the Latimer Model. They are able to make their audience care; but more than that, they are able to compel their audience to act (and not out of obligation, but by choice). They can be depended upon to accomplish the most complex persuasion challenges—they persuade in situations that require a high degree of involvement and an equally high level of change.

Mastering Each Skill

In addition to thinking holistically about your communication skill level, we break down these levels into each of the four skill areas. After all, a key element to the Latimer Model is thinking about communication as a set of discrete, perfectible skills that can be practiced and improved separately. While many of these skills play off each other, it is likely that you are stronger in one skill than another. Identifying these strengths and weaknesses allows you to work more precisely and intensely on the areas in which you need improvement. (What's more, even when you've earned Executive Standard work for one presentation, it doesn't mean you can rest on your laurels; you'll still need to practice the model to consistently achieve results.)

Let's break down what each standard looks like across these four skill areas.

Assess. Before you even start to pull together your slide deck or gather up your best anecdotes, you need to understand the context in which you are speaking and analyze the aspect of your presentation that will be most effective. What does your audience care about the most? What do they need from this communication?

If you are at the Professional Standard of this skill, you understand what your audience will be listening for: do they want hard data or personal stories? Are they an audience that needs to approve a decision, or execute a decision?

At the Leadership Standard, you can identify your audience's priorities, and can speak to how your proposal fits into them.

At the Executive Standard, audience objections are identified and resolved, and consensus is built through leadership.

Key questions for improvement:

- Who is going to be in the room?
- What does my audience care about?
- What's my credibility?
- What is the most effective way to structure my message?

Message. Once you've gathered your information, you'll need to craft a message that is powerful, persuasive, and holds your audience's attention.

At the Professional Standard, you achieve a clear, well-organized presentation that is easy to follow and ably gets across the key points. Every audience member will leave the room knowing what you need—but may not yet be convinced to do it. While the message is clear, it doesn't feel specific to the audience, and the benefits to them aren't elucidated.

At the Leadership Standard, your well-organized presentation also targets key areas of interest to your audience and convinces them that the issue at hand is vital.

At the Executive Standard, each piece of information presented feels important, necessary, and persuasive. Relevant anecdotes and examples bring the issue to life. Audience members leave with a clear sense of what needs to be done, when it needs to be done, and why. Listeners feel connected and inspired.

Key questions for improvement:

- What is the goal of this communication?
- What is the key information this specific audience needs to know?
- What are the main objections to my proposal?
- How do I make my audience feel connected to my subject?

Document. You have a strong, well-crafted message. Now you need to pull together the visual support that will reinforce that message.

At the Professional Standard, your slides are clean and coherent—minimal typos or inconsistencies to distract the audience. They follow the logical progression of your presentation.

At the Leadership Standard, your slides will make the key ideas of your presentation stand out. This visual representation will help your audience retain your message.

At the Executive Standard, your slides not only make your key ideas stand out, they sell those ideas. The visual presentation of your ideas engages the audience and speaks to their interests and needs.

Key questions for improvement:

- Is the slide content easy for the audience to comprehend while also listening to me?
- Will my audience be distracted in any way by this slide—by a typo, by having to read long sentences, by having to decode a too-small graphic?
- Does every slide express a key idea?
- Do my visual elements serve the message?

Deliver. In many ways, this is the most intimidating aspect of communicating: standing up in front of an audience and speaking with confidence and authenticity.

At the Professional level, you've worked to eliminate most if not all verbal pauses, you've calmed your fidgets, and you use eye contact to connect with the room.

At the Leadership level, you use speech patterns to emphasize key points—inflection, pauses, signposting statements (such as, "The key point here is..."), bullet points.

At the Executive level, your command of the room and the material is evident. Objections and questions are handled calmly and thoroughly, and you are clearly as willing to listen as to speak. Your demeanor and vocabulary are powerful and appropriate for the message.

Key questions for improvement:

- Am I speaking in a way that is natural and true to myself?
- Am I connecting with my audience?
- Am I emphasizing the key points in a way that is memorable?
- Does my energy match my message?

Three Simple Concepts

I believe that The Latimer Group frameworks can transform communication—for individuals, teams, and entire organizations. If this seems lofty, it is also grounded in years of practical engagement and application of the concepts. What is required to kickstart this transformation? Nothing more than attitude, commitment, and training.

When we think about how to become better communicators, we often think about the tools we use—our data, our PowerPoint deck, our posture and poise. And these are crucial. But the real keys to sustained, long-term improvement and success as a communicator might surprise you—in part because they are simple, easy to implement, and available to everyone.

Think of training for an athletic competition. You have your gear, your teammates, your past experience to draw on. But to succeed, you also need to set ambitious goals, must adhere to a training plan, and need to practice assiduously until you've perfected all the necessary skills. Otherwise, you'll struggle to push yourself beyond your comfort zone—and to truly advance to a higher level of competition.

The same concepts apply to honing your communication skills. You need to turn on that mental switch that says, "I want to improve, and I want to be the best I can be." When you turn on this switch, you activate three important spheres:

Attitude: Positive and proactive. Every opportunity to speak becomes an opportunity to persuade your audience. A meeting with colleagues, a phone call with a client, or a formal presentation; no communication is without a challenge to be clear, be confident, and be persuasive.

Commitment: Total and persistent. Challenge yourself on every skill and be deliberate about how you seek to improve.

Training: Thorough and long-term. Ask your colleagues for feedback, and provide constructive, honest feedback in return. Seek out mentors—and recognize that as your communication improves, so will your career trajectory.

Amplifying the Change

Individual training can make a huge difference in the way that one employee communicates with her colleagues or clients. But an organization truly sees the benefits of persuasive communication when the Latimer Model frameworks and goals are embedded into an organization's professional development curriculum and overall culture. When these concepts are applied company-wide, it allows for greater practice, feedback, and reinforcement, which creates a culture of continuous improvement and refinement of communication skills.

In my practice, I have seen how committed leadership, a common vocabulary, and deliberate use of feedback can help cascade the effects of purposeful communication from top to bottom of an organization. In turn, outcome-oriented and persuasive communication can bring greater employee satisfaction, efficiency, innovation, and profitability.

I've seen directly the impact of implementing a company-wide communication framework that extends from the top down. When a company starts by enrolling executives in The Latimer Group workshops, so that leadership experiences the curriculum, the vocabulary, and the system directly and incorporates them into their own communication, the return for other employees goes up exponentially. When we work at these companies, we don't hear things like, "My boss tells me I can't structure my presentation like this"; "Has my boss gone through this training?"; "Are you sure we're allowed to do this?"

For example, we engaged with Company A and Company B at almost the same time. At Company A, the very first employees we worked with were the ones who hired us—the three managing directors who wanted us to work with their teams. When it came time for their reports to take workshops, they were unfailingly more committed, more engaged, and more willing to be vulnerable and take risks—because they knew their bosses had already done so, had already made the vocabulary of the workshops commonplace through the organization, and had already improved their own communication.

At Company B, the two executives who hired us were enthusiastic about what we teach and couldn't wait for us to start running workshops. But when I suggested that they go through one of the first workshops, they both demurred; they trusted us, they didn't have time, and they didn't need to improve their communication anyway. When we started to work with their team, we still saw a great impact on the communication but progress was slower. People were warier of the vocabulary and the suggestions we made because they were encountering them for the first time, and the participants were both resentful that their bosses hadn't bothered with the curriculum and worried that they wouldn't support the changes we suggested.

When frameworks and curriculum are instituted from the top down, everyone feels more confident, more committed, and benefits from ongoing reinforcement. Organizational communication *can* improve from the bottom up, but the return on investment will always be faster and greater when it comes from the top down.

Transforming the World

I believe deeply in the power of persuasive communication to enhance and improve the professional lives of individuals and their organizations. But can we take these concepts even further? I believe the answer is yes. I believe that the precepts of persuasive communication—connection, clarity, respect, empathy—can transform entire industries and even the world.

Think about the purpose of persuasive communication: to elucidate a goal, to make your audience care about that goal, and to inspire them to act toward achieving that goal. Throughout this book, I've talked about business goals—getting approval for a budget, selling a product, arguing for a promotion. But the same tools and concepts can help achieve personal goals as well, from making decisions for your family to discussing politics to supporting your church or your favorite cause.

These goals can be achieved by setting some of the same priorities as you would in business communication.

Connection: At the root of all communication, you always need to find a way to connect to the other person you are speaking with in order to find alignment. It is difficult to inspire people if they don't feel connected to you in some way.

Clarity: Has anyone ever said, in any context, "I wish you would be a little less clear about what you want or need"? Cultivating the ability to communicate clearly and simply is invaluable, no matter who you are talking to or why.

Respect and empathy: Use your active listening skills to demonstrate your sincere interest in another person's perspective and insights. Not only will you learn something, but you'll more likely find a receptive audience for your own thoughts and perspective.

Can we all be more thoughtful, more purposeful, more persuasive in our communication? Yes, and the more we set out to do so, the easier, the quicker, and the more instinctive it becomes. We inhabit a noisy, distracted world, and the rules of success have changed. To make an impact, we need to break out of the messenger mindset. We need to be goal-oriented and purposeful in our communication. We need to simplify and summarize. We need to *connect*.

Imagine a world in which we listen to each other, we speak honestly and directly, and we seek out dialogue, not monologic argumentation. That's the world I imagine with *Persuaded*.

About the Author

Dean M. Brenner
President and Founder, The Latimer Group

Dean Brenner is a recognized expert in powerful communication skills. Since 2003, Dean has coached and trained executives, sales teams, leaders, managers, and technical experts in a wide range of industries on the topics of persuasive communication, effective message development, and leadership. The Latimer Group serves a global client base on five continents, with active relationships throughout North America and across the globe.

Dean's approach to coaching and training is based on listening closely to the client's need, and then drawing on all aspects of his background to coach in the most effective way possible. Dean works with his clients from the perspective of an executive coach, an athlete, a leader of teams, a member of teams, a mentor to Olympic athletes, and as a husband and father. He focuses on ideas that will help his clients communicate simply, clearly, and powerfully.

Dean is a published author, and his second title, *Sharing the Sandbox: Building and Leading World-Class Teams in the 21st Century* was published in May 2012. His first title was, *Move the World: Persuade Your Audience, Change Minds, and Achieve Your Goals* (Wiley, 2007). Dean is also a popular keynote speaker, presenting on topics ranging from leadership and persuasive communication to team dynamics and high performance.

In addition to his work with The Latimer Group, Dean served as chairman and team leader of the US Olympic Sailing Program for the 2008 Olympic Games in Beijing and the 2012 Olympic Games in London. Prior to his Olympic leadership role, Dean was an athlete on the US Sailing Team for four years and an alternate on the 2000 Olympic Team. He is a six-time national and North American champion.

Dean earned an MBA in finance from the Olin School of Business at Babson College, and an MA in Shakespearian Literature from the University of Warwick, England. He also holds a BA from Georgetown University.

The Latimer Group: Who We Are

The Latimer Group began in 2002 with a singular vision: a skill-based, objectively assessed approach to persuasive communication, one that allowed *anyone* to become a powerful, next-level speaker.

The response was immediate. The ever-increasing complexity of the business world meant that effective communication wasn't just a valuable skill; it had become invaluable. Clients wanted and needed a clear, refined curriculum that was easy to implement and that made improving communication across multiple platforms measurable, achievable, and replicable.

Over the years, the team has grown. Each new team member helped hone and strengthen The Latimer Group vision, adding value and reach. And every team member brought in a new set of skills and perspectives: competitive sailing, literature, education, psychology, sales and marketing, eLearning design, teaching.

Through each of our unique perspectives, we have managed to grow and evolve; to adapt to new circumstances, new contexts, and new opportunities while remaining true to the original vision. Our ethos is one of customization and collaboration with our clients and with each other. We take an evolutionary approach to our methods, constantly engaging with and interrogating our teaching frameworks and techniques. We rely on our collective experience. As of this writing, we've taught more than twelve hundred workshops for more than ten thousand participants, and coached hundreds of leaders, directors, managers, and individual contributors.

We believe in a world where great communication is possible. We believe that anyone can become a more effective, persuasive speaker. And we believe that great communication can transform an organization and change the world.

The Latimer Group team:

Dean M. Brenner: President and Founder

Whitney C. Sweeney: Director of Client Relations

Hannah A. Morris: Director of Assessment and Advancement

Kendra E. Raguckas: Director of Instructional Design & Technology

Daniel J. Cooney: Director of Business Development

Jordan DeFreitas: Marketing and Operations Associate

Acknowledgments

Many people—far too many to mention here—have provided great support and encouragement for this project, for The Latimer Group, and for me. But a few deserve some special mention:

- My colleagues at The Latimer Group—Whitney Sweeney, Hannah Morris, Kendra Raguckas, Dan Cooney, and Jordan DeFreitas—are as strong a team as a guy like me could hope for. You inspire me and hold me accountable every day and make me better than I could ever be on my own.
- My former colleague Amy Fenollosa, who was a major driver behind this book and who brought great energy to her work with our clients.
- The Latimer Group's Board of Advisors—Tom Lips, Phil Bonanno, Mike Davis, Bryan Gildenberg, Bill Goggins, Alix Hahn, and Josh Levine. Every one of you is a powerhouse in every sense of the word in your intellect, your spirit, and your generosity. I am forever in your debt.
- Gerald Sindell, who has been my "idea whisperer" ever since we first spoke in 2005. You have guided me flawlessly through two book projects. But beyond that, your idea generation process has driven The Latimer Group's content creation for the last fifteen years.

- My writing partner Andrea Thompson, who is as talented a writer as any I have ever met. Your ability to always find the correct word and tone is uncanny. Thank you for being a quiet but powerful part of The Latimer Group's success.
- Our blog master, the endlessly helpful Brett Slater. You help us find our voice every single day, and we are forever grateful.
- And, finally, to my wife Emily, my son Zachary, and my daughter, Kate. It is simply not possible to love you more than I do. Everything I do, I do for you.

Appendix

CHAPTER 3: ASSESS EFFECTIVENESS REVIEW
Awareness & Listen

- Did I generate the impact I wanted?
- Did I notice a situational shift in my audience?
- If so, did I adjust effectively?
- What was my mindset before the meeting/presentation?
- Did it affect my communication?

Analyze

- Did I assess my audience effectively?
- Did I provide enough background and/or translation?
- Did I anticipate and address my audience's goals and objections?
- Did I learn anything new about my audience?
- Did I feel confident in my credibility?
- Did the audience listen actively?
- Did they ask questions and engage in discussion?
- Did I assess the opportunity correctly?
- Was my preparation comprehensive?
- Did I maximize my leverage?

CHAPTER 4: MESSAGE EFFECTIVENESS REVIEW
Organization
The OPEN

- Did the opening device grab the audience's attention?
- Did the open provide context for the audience?

- Was there a high-level summary with a clear statement of problem, solution, and ask?
- Were the key points laid out?

The CONTENT

- Did each chapter address one key point?
- Was there an appropriate amount of data and detail?
- Was each chapter introduced and recapped effectively?
- Were transitions between chapters logical?

The CLOSE

- Did the close reiterate the high-level summary included in the open?
- Did the audience leave with a clear call-to-action?

Information

The WHAT

- Was the problem/issue/situation described clearly?
- Was there a clear recommendation or solution?
- Were the key points clear and thoroughly developed?
- Was there a specific ask of the audience?

The WHY

- Did the presenter give the audience sufficient context without too much detail?
- Did the presenter demonstrate value and relevance to the audience?
- Did the presenter enable the audience to care?

The WHY NOT

- Did the presenter anticipate and answer questions?
- Did the presenter address and resolve likely objections?
- Did the presenter state the risk of inaction?

The HOW

- Were the main points supporting the recommendation clear?
- Was the structure of the recommendation compelling?
- Did the presenter quantify the benefit? The cost? The risk?

The NEXT

- Were the next steps clearly stated?
- Were accountability and timeline addressed?
- Was the audience given clear action items (if appropriate)?

CHAPTER 5: DOCUMENT EFFECTIVENESS REVIEW

Design

- Did the document follow a template?
- Did the order of the slides/sections follow the arc of the story?
- Did the layout and formatting make information stand out?
- Did the document exhibit appropriate word economy?
- Was there an appropriate balance of visuals and text?
- Was there a good use of white space and contrast?
- Was the document visually appealing?
- Was the document visually consistent?
- Was the design effective?

Content

- Was there enough context and big picture?
- Did the document have the appropriate level of detail?
- Was each component essential to the document?
- Was there enough of a business case?
- Were benefits, costs, and/or risks clearly addressed?
- Was there a clear call-to-action?

- Did the images create meaningful associations for the audience?
- Did the graphics illustrate key points effectively?
- Was the key point in each slide/section obvious?

CHAPTER 6: DELIVER EFFECTIVENESS REVIEW

Body Language & Voice

- Did the presenter have strong, open posture?
- Was the movement purposeful?
- Were the hand gestures meaningful?
- Did the presenter convey appropriate energy and emotion?
- Did the presenter engage the audience with meaningful eye contact?
- Did the presenter interact to the right extent with the slides?
- Did the presenter speak at a consistently audible volume?
- Did the presenter enunciate and project clearly?
- Was the pace appropriate?
- Did the presenter pause with silence instead of verbal pauses?
- Did the presenter modulate tone to emphasize and engage?
- Was inflection used appropriately for statements and questions?

Verbal Language

- Did the presenter speak "in periods, not commas"?
- Did the presenter use strong vocabulary?
- Did the presenter avoid undermining language?
- Did the presenter avoid filler words?
- Did the presenter speak in bullet points?
- Did the presenter verbally highlight key points?

- Did the presenter pause and/or repeat for emphasis?
- Did the presenter connect with the audience using humor or storytelling?
- Did the presenter engage the audience with real or rhetorical questions?
- Did the presenter strike the right balance of "I" and "we"?
- Did the presenter use WIIFY ("What's In It For You") statements?
- Did the presenter define terms or acronyms that may be unfamiliar to the audience?

References

Brown, Brené. *Daring Greatly: How the Courage to Be Vulnerable Transforms the Way We Live, Love, Parent, and Lead.* New York: Avery, 2012.

Cuddy, Amy. *Presence: Bringing Your Boldest Self to Your Biggest Challenges.* New York: Little, Brown and Company, 2015.

Hewlett, Sylvia Ann. *Executive Presence: The Missing Link Between Merit and Success.* New York: Harper Business, 2014.

Kaiser Family Foundation. "Loneliness and Social Isolation in the United States, the United Kingdom, and Japan: An International Survey." August 30, 2018. https://www.kff.org/report-section/loneliness-and-social-isolation-in-the-united-states-the-united-kingdom-and-japan-an-international-survey-introduction/

Pink, Daniel. *To Sell is Human: The Surprising Truth About Moving Others.* New York: Riverhead Books, 2012.

Sinek, Simon. *Start With Why: How Great Leaders Inspire Everyone to Take Action.* New York: Portfolio, 2009.

Voss, Chris, with Tahl Raz. *Never Split the Difference: Negotiating As If Your Life Depended On It.* New York: Harper Business, 2016.

CPSIA information can be obtained
at www.ICGtesting.com
Printed in the USA
JSHW051155191121
20598JS00001B/2

9 781662 901584